WORLD
HISTORY SERIES ■■■

The Age of Pericles

Titles in the World History Series

The Age of Feudalism
The Age of Pericles
The American Frontier
The American Revolution
Ancient Greece
The Ancient Near East
Architecture
Aztec Civilization
Caesar's Conquest of Gaul
The Crusades
The Cuban Revolution
The Early Middle Ages
Egypt of the Pharaohs
Elizabethan England
The End of the Cold War
The French and Indian War
The French Revolution
The Glorious Revolution
The Great Depression
Greek and Roman Theater
Hitler's Reich

The Hundred Years' War
The Inquisition
The Italian Renaissance
The Late Middle Ages
The Lewis and Clark
    Expedition
Modern Japan
The Punic Wars
The Reformation
The Relocation of the
    North American Indian
The Roman Empire
The Roman Republic
The Russian Revolution
The Scientific Revolution
The Spread of Islam
Traditional Africa
Traditional Japan
The Travels of Marco Polo
The Wars of the Roses
Women's Suffrage

WORLD HISTORY SERIES ■ ■ ■

The Age of Pericles

by
Don Nardo

Lucent Books, P.O. Box 289011, San Diego, CA 92198-9011

Library of Congress Cataloging-in-Publication Data

Nardo, Don, 1947–
    The age of Pericles / by Don Nardo
        p. cm.—(World history series)
    Includes bibliographical references and index.
    ISBN 1-56006-303-3 (alk. paper)
    1. Greece—History—Athenian supremacy, 479–431 B.C.—
Juvenile literature. 2. Pericles, 499–429 B.C.—Juvenile literature.
I.Title. II. Series.
DF227.N37   1996
938—dc20   95-25422
                                                                CIP
                                                                 AC

Contents

Foreword

Each year on the first day of school, nearly every history teacher faces the task of explaining why his or her students should study history. One logical answer to this question is that exploring what happened in our past explains how the things we often take for granted—our customs, ideas, and institutions—came to be. As statesman and historian Winston Churchill put it, "Every nation or group of nations has its own tale to tell. Knowledge of the trials and struggles is necessary to all who would comprehend the problems, perils, challenges, and opportunities which confront us today." Thus, a study of history puts modern ideas and institutions in perspective. For example, though the founders of the United States were talented and creative thinkers, they clearly did not invent the concept of democracy. Instead, they adapted some democratic ideas that had originated in ancient Greece and with which the Romans, the British, and others had experimented. An exploration of these cultures, then, reveals their very real connection to us through institutions that continue to shape our daily lives.

Another reason often given for studying history is the idea that lessons exist in the past from which contemporary societies can benefit and learn. This idea, although controversial, has always been an intriguing one for historians. Those that agree that society can benefit from the past often quote philosopher George Santayana's famous statement, "Those who cannot remember the past are condemned to repeat it." Historians who ascribe to Santayana's philosophy believe that, for example, studying the events that led up to the major world wars or other significant historical events would allow society to chart a different and more favorable course in the future.

Just as difficult as convincing students to realize the importance of studying history is the search for useful and interesting supplementary materials that present historical events in a context that can be easily understood. The volumes in Lucent Books' World History Series attempt to present a broad, balanced, and penetrating view of the march of history. Ancient Egypt's important wars and rulers, for example, are presented against the rich and colorful backdrop of Egyptian religious, social, and cultural developments. The series engages the reader by enhancing historical events with these cultural contexts. For example, in *Ancient Greece*, the text covers the role of women in that society. Slavery is discussed in *The Roman Empire*, as well as how slaves earned their freedom. The numerous and varied aspects of everyday life in these and other societies are explored in each volume of the series. Additionally, the series covers the major political, cultural, and philosophical ideas as the torch of civilization is passed from ancient Mesopotamia and Egypt, through Greece, Rome, Medieval Europe, and other world cultures, to the modern day.

The material in the series is formatted in a thorough, precise, and organized manner. Each volume offers the reader a comprehensive and clearly written overview of an important historical event or period. The topic under discussion is placed in a broad historical context. For example, *The Italian Renaissance* begins with a discussion of the High Middle Ages and the loss of central control that allowed certain Italian cities to develop artistically. The book ends by looking forward to the Reformation and interpreting the societal changes that grew out of the Renaissance. Thus, students are not only involved in an historical era, but also enveloped by the events leading up to that era and the events following it.

One important and unique feature in the World History Series is the primary and secondary source quotations that richly supplement each volume. These quotes are useful in a number of ways. First, they allow students access to sources they would not normally be exposed to because of the difficulty and obscurity of the original source. The quotations range from interesting anecdotes to farsighted cultural perspectives and are drawn from historical witnesses both past and present. Second, the quotes demonstrate how and where historians themselves derive their information on the past as they strive to reach a consensus on historical events. Lastly, all of the quotes are footnoted, familiarizing students with the citation process and allowing them to verify quotes and/or look up the original source if the quote piques their interest.

Finally, the books in the World History Series provide a detailed launching point for further research. Each book contains a bibliography specifically geared toward student research. A second, annotated bibliography introduces students to all the sources the author consulted when compiling the book. A chronology of important dates gives students an overview, at a glance, of the topic covered. Where applicable, a glossary of terms is included.

In short, the series is designed not only to acquaint readers with the basics of history, but also to make them aware that their lives are a part of an ongoing human saga. Perhaps they will then come to the same realization as famed historian Arnold Toynbee. In his monumental work, *A Study of History*, he wrote about becoming aware of history flowing through him in a mighty current, and of his own life "welling like a wave in the flow of this vast tide."

Important Dates in the History of the Age of Pericles

B.C.	1200	1152	1104	1056	1008	960	912	864	816

B.C.

ca. 1200
The Mycenaean Greeks, including contingents from Athens and Sparta, sack the city of Troy in Asia Minor.

ca. 1100
The warlike Dorians invade the Mycenaean towns, plunging Greece into a cultural dark age.

ca. 800
The dark age ends and the Archaic Age, a period marked by increasing prosperity and the rise of city-states across Greece, begins.

ca. 800–600
A mode of warfare centered around the hoplite, or heavily armored infantry soldier, develops in Greece; Sparta's army emerges as the best and most feared in the land.

594
An Athenian aristocrat named Solon initiates several political reforms, setting Athens on the path to democracy.

ca. 520
Sparta is acknowledged as the dominant city-state in the Peloponnesus, the large peninsula making up the southern third of Greece.

507
Under the political reformer Cleisthenes, Athens becomes a full-fledged democracy, the first in world history.

490
Athenian hoplites defeat a force of invading Persians on the plain of Marathon, northeast of Athens.

479
A united Greek army completes the destruction of a second Persian invasion force at Plataea, in southern Boeotia.

478
The Delian League, an alliance of city-states led by Athens, is established; the period later variously referred to as the Fifty Years, the golden age of Athens, and the Age of Pericles begins.

472
The Athenian leader Themistocles is ostracized and banished.

469
The popular and capable Athenian general Cimon defeats the Persians along the Eurymedon River in southern Asia Minor, giving the Greeks undisputed control of the Aegean Sea; the island of Naxos tries to resign from the Delian League but Cimon compels it to

remain by the use of military force, marking the beginning of the league's transition into an Athenian empire.

464
Sparta is leveled by a massive earthquake; taking advantage of the disaster, the Spartan helots, or agricultural serfs, rebel.

461
Cimon is ostracized; his rival and successor, Ephialtes, is assassinated, leaving Pericles the most powerful leader in Athens; Athens makes alliances with Sparta's enemies, Argos and Thessaly; the Athenians institute domestic democratic reforms, including payment for jury duty.

460
Accepting the invitation of a Lybian king to help liberate the Egyptians from Persian rule, Athens sends two hundred ships to Egypt.

457
An Athenian army clashes with a force of Spartans and Peloponnesian allies at Tanagra, in southern Boeotia; two months later, after the Spartans have returned home, Athens defeats Thebes and its allies at Oenophyta, near Tanagra.

| 768 | 720 | 672 | 624 | 576 | 528 | 480 | 432 | 384 | 338 |

454
Athens's Egyptian expedition meets disaster as the Persians crush the rebellion in Egypt; Pericles transfers the Delian League's treasury from Delos to Athens, prompting protests by many league members.

451
Cimon, back from exile, arranges for a five-year truce between Athens and Sparta.

449
Athens concludes the Peace of Callias with Persia, ending many decades of war between the Greeks and the Persians.

446
Athens and Sparta conclude the Thirty Years Peace, agreeing to stay out of each other's sphere of influence.

443
Athens establishes a cleruchy, or state-sponsored settlement, at Thurii in southern Italy; Pericles' chief political opponent, Thucydides of Alopece, is banished, leaving Pericles supreme in Athens.

440–439
Pericles besieges and subjugates the island polis of Samos after its rebellion against Athens, setting an example that discourages other Aegean states from challenging Athenian supremacy.

438
The Parthenon, the magnificent temple dedicated to the goddess Athena, is completed atop Athens's Acropolis.

435
A civil war erupts between oligarchs and democrats on the island of Corcyra, off Greece's northwestern coast, a conflict that will soon draw in both Corinth and Athens and lead to a larger war.

432
The Propylaea, the splendid entranceway of the Acropolis complex, is completed; Athens imposes a trade embargo on the city-state of Megara.

431
Sparta declares war on Athens, initiating the Peloponnesian War, which engulfs all of Greece; the Spartans and their allies invade Attica, and the Athenians take shelter behind newly constructed city walls.

430
A deadly plague strikes Athens.

429
Pericles contracts the plague and dies.

422
The combatants negotiate a truce, the Peace of Nicias; but the agreement soon proves a failure and the war rages on.

413
Athens suffers the worst military disaster in its history in a failed attempt to conquer the city of Syracuse in Sicily.

405
The Spartans defeat the Athenians at Aegospotami, near the Hellespont, closing off Athens's life-giving grain route to the Black Sea.

404
Athens surrenders; Sparta forces it to tear down its defensive walls, abolish its democracy, and install an oligarchy.

371
Thebes defeats Sparta at Leuctra, in central Boeotia, forever eliminating Sparta as a major Greek power.

338
King Philip II of Macedonia defeats a united Greek army led by Athens and Thebes at Chaeronea, in Boeotia, robbing the war-weary Greek city-states of their last vestiges of power and independence.

The Worst Along with the Best

In the fourth century B.C. the Greeks longingly began referring to a part of the preceding century—roughly five decades—as the *Pentekontaetia*, the Fifty Years. In modern times, scholars came to call this period, lasting from 479 to 431 B.C., the "golden age" of Athens. It was the brief but glorious age when that city-state, the largest and

The profoundly influential politician Pericles oversaw most of Athens's domestic and foreign policies for more than thirty years.

most influential in Greece, reached its political and cultural zenith. The grand achievements of a single gifted generation of Athenian artists, architects, sculptors, playwrights, philosophers, and democratic reformers have awed and inspired every succeeding human generation.

Later generations came to call this fruitful period the Age of Pericles in recognition of the politician/statesman/general who dominated the Athenian state for much of the Fifty Years. "Great as Athens had been when he became her leader," wrote the later Greek/Roman historian Plutarch, "he made her the greatest and richest of all cities."[1] Looking back on Athens's artistic, literary, and material splendor, many modern scholars have tended to emphasize the cultural legacies of both the city and its leading citizen. As classical scholar Victor Ehrenberg describes it, in the bulk of modern studies "Pericles and his times have been regarded as the very fulfillment of human endeavor and cultural harmony."[2]

But cultural achievement was only part of the legacy of the Periclean age. The *Pentekontaetia* was also a time of complex political turmoil and bloody military strife among the Greek city-states. These years saw ever-worsening relations between the two leading Greek states, Athens and

Athens's magnificent Acropolis, including the famous Parthenon, as it appeared at the height of the Periclean age (right background), was dedicated to the city's patron goddess, Athena.

Sparta, and their respective federations of allies. A generation of animosity and on-and-off fighting, much of it instigated by Pericles and his supporters, finally led to the outbreak of the Peloponnesian War in 431 B.C. This terrifying and devastating twenty-seven-year-long conflict engulfed and exhausted the entire Greek world and ended Athens's glorious golden age.

Thus, to achieve a realistic and balanced view of the Periclean age and of Pericles himself, it is necessary to examine both sides of the issue. In addition to the familiar, culturally splendid and politically enlightened aspect, almost every famous event or achievement of the period had a darker and less admirable side. For instance, one of the events that marked the height of the Fifty Years was the construction of the magnificent Parthenon and other religious temples in the heart of Athens. This was a marvelous accomplishment, to be sure. But it is often overlooked that these great public edifices were built with funds diverted from Athens's allies under very controversial circumstances. Many Greeks accused

Athens, and Pericles in particular, of questionable conduct and even of outright theft.

In this and other instances, emphasizing the admirable and constructive aspects while glossing over the darker ones only serves to distort twentieth-century perceptions of the Periclean age. To be realistic, Pericles and the other Greek leaders of his day should be seen as human beings who accomplished great deeds but also made their share of mistakes and paid the price for those errors. "The greatness of [Pericles] and his age," says Ehrenberg, "will emerge even more convincingly if shadows show off the light, and men of flesh and blood replace the pale idols of pure harmony and perfection."[3]

From this balanced perspective, Pericles, the symbol of Greece's greatest age, emerges as a complex and fascinating individual. On the one hand, he was a champion of democracy. "Our system is called a democracy, for it respects the majority and not the few," he stated in his most famous speech, which was preserved by his contemporary, the Greek historian

Thucydides. "Nor . . . is there any bar in poverty or low social status to a man who can do the state some service. It is as free men that we conduct our public life."[4] On the other hand, by expertly manipulating the system to maintain his own power, Pericles dominated the Athenian democracy for decades. Through his powerful oratory and his shrewd political dealings, he managed to get himself reelected repeatedly, always at the expense of other worthy individuals. Even Thucydides, who greatly admired him, wrote that "Athens, though in the name of democracy, was in fact coming to be ruled by her first citizen."[5]

Similarly, on the one hand Pericles was a cultural champion who encouraged artists and erected grand public buildings. On the other, he was an ardent imperialist who was willing to expand Athens's power at the expense of its neighbors and through the use of any means necessary, including threats, bribery, and naked military force. Some scholars credit him with leading Athens to greatness and then, in one of the ironies of history, provoking the Peloponnesian War, which set Athens and the rest of Greece on the path to destruction.

Thus, the Periclean age was a period of cultural greatness and a complex and turbulent age, as well. It was an age characterized and driven by both the best and the worst attributes of ancient Greece's remarkable civilization. In the glaring light of modern historical examination, the search for truth and balance must focus on the worst along with the best.

Chapter

1 Seeds of Bitter Rivalry: The Long Prelude to the Classic Age

The Periclean age and the terrible Peloponnesian War that erupted from it took place in what modern historians call the Classic Age of Greece. This was the period, lasting roughly from 500 to 300 B.C., in which ancient Greek civilization reached its military, cultural, and intellectual zenith. It was an age when Greece, led by Athens, produced magnificent art, architecture, and literature that has amazed and inspired the world ever since. But it was also an age of bitter civil strife that exhausted and tore apart the leading Greek city-states at the very moment of their greatest glory and ultimately doomed them to oblivion.

Clearly, the dominant political factor behind both the Periclean age and the subsequent war was the mutual distrust and rivalry between the city-states of Athens and Sparta and their respective allies. This bitter rivalry was a long time in the making. The seeds that would bear simultaneously such *pro*ductive and *de*structive fruit in the time of Pericles were planted long before the famous statesman first moved Athenians with his oratory. To understand how Athens and Sparta came to dominate the Greek world and eventually to set it on the road to ruin, we must begin more than a thousand years before Pericles was born.

Athens and Sparta in the Bronze Age

Athens and Sparta were two of the oldest towns on the Greek mainland, the mountainous, rugged, arid peninsula projecting southward from Europe into the clear blue waters of the eastern Mediterranean Sea. Sparta was located in the southern part of the Peloponnesus, the large peninsula that comprises the lower third of the mainland. Athens rested near the western edge of Attica, a smaller peninsula jutting eastward into the Aegean Sea, the island-studded Mediterranean inlet that separates Greece from Asia Minor, what is now Turkey.

Both Athens and Sparta were founded sometime early in Greece's first civilized era, which lasted from about 3000 to 1100 B.C. Historians refer to this period as the Greek Bronze Age because the people used tools and weapons made of bronze, a tough alloy of copper and tin. At the time, Athens and Sparta, like most other major settlements, were small fortress-towns ruled by kings and dominated by palaces surrounded by massive stone defensive walls. Later scholars came to call the inhabitants of these early mainland sites "Mycenaean" after Mycenae, the strongest of the fortress-towns, which was located in the northeastern Peloponnesus.

For centuries, the Mycenaeans were dominated, both culturally and politically, by the Minoans, another early Greek people that held sway on the large island of Crete and on most of the smaller Aegean islands. The Minoans possessed powerful fleets of ships for both trade and warfare. These vessels enforced Crete's economic and political supremacy in the eastern Mediterranean sphere. Bowing to this supremacy, the Athenians, Spartans, and other Mycenaeans adopted Minoan dress styles and social customs and apparently also paid the Minoans periodic tribute, or large sums of money. The Minoans may have demanded other forms of payment, too, as suggested by the Greek myth of Theseus. According to this legend, mainland Athens was forced periodically to send young men and women as captives to the Cretan capital of Knossus. There, the victims were sacrificed to the Minotaur, a fearsome creature that was half man and half bull. That the Minoan religion was heavily dominated by bull worship no

ANCIENT GREECE

Greek areas

The legendary hero Theseus rescues a group of Athenian captives from certain death in the Cretan labyrinth, the mazelike building where the fearsome Minotaur dwelled.

doubt accounts for the form devised for the monster.

Minoan supremacy ceased unexpectedly when the volcanic island of Thera, located some seventy miles north of Crete, erupted, perhaps about 1500 B.C. According to scholar Rodney Castleden:

> Major earthquakes with their epicenters on Thera would have caused significant damage to Knossus and other Minoan sites on Crete. The final eruption would have been experienced as a multiple disaster at the Minoan sites. The initial damage to walls and foundations by blast and earthquake was followed by a towering tsunami, or "tidal" wave, which would have washed across the northern coastal lowlands, destroying the principal Minoan harbor towns. . . . After the waters of the . . . tsunami receded, a great cloud of white [volcanic] ash . . . covered the whole of central and eastern Crete . . . enough to put the farmland out of production for several years and paralyze the Minoan economy.[6]

This disaster did not destroy the Minoans. But it weakened them enough to allow the Mycenaeans to overrun and take control of Crete and the islands during the succeeding generation.

The Trojan War

The Mycenaeans, the natives of Athens and Sparta among them, then dominated Aegean trade and politics for three centuries. During these years the Mycenaean

The Foremost Kingdom of Greece

Although few traces remain today of the Mycenaean fortresses at Athens and Sparta, it is likely that they closely resembled the better-preserved citadel at Mycenae, as described in this excerpt from The Legend of Odysseus, *by historian Peter Connolly.*

"The citadel at Mycenae was built on a hillock overlooking the Plain of Argos. Traces of at least four major roads have been found leading to the citadel identifying it as the most important center in the area and supporting Homer's claim that it was the foremost kingdom of Greece. The citadel is crowned by a palace with a great columned hall known as a megaron. The temples and the graves of the early kings are further down the slope. The citadel is surrounded by massive walls between 5.5 and 7.5 meters [18 and 24 feet] thick. Some of the stones are so huge that later Greeks believed that they must have been built by Cyclopses [mythical giants]. At one point the walls are still 8.25 meters [26 feet] high and may originally have been as much as 12 meters [38 feet] high. The main gate is known as the Lion Gate from the two lions carved above the lintel [beam forming the gate's top]. It was defended by a bastion [fortified wall] from which missiles could be hurled at the unshielded side of any attackers. There is a similar gate in the north wall."

A nineteenth-century drawing of the ruins of the citadel of Mycenae, which, like those of Athens and Sparta, first appeared during Greece's Bronze Age.

fortresses reached their height of power and splendor. Historian Michael Wood adds details:

> For the mainland palaces, the period between 1300 and [about] 1250 B.C. was the greatest period of Mycenaean building. . . . At this time tremendous fortifications were completed at Gla, Tiryns, Mycenae, Athens, and at scores of lesser sites.[7]

The kings of these cities, as well as of Sparta, Pylos, and others, looked to the nearby coasts of Asia Minor as potential sources of new wealth. What they could not acquire through bargaining, they took by force.

Probably the largest and certainly the most famous of the Mycenaean war raids took place in about 1200 B.C.: the siege and sack of the independent trading city of Troy, located on the northwestern coast of Asia Minor. The exciting events that supposedly occurred during and immediately following this expedition were the basis for two epic poems, the *Iliad* and the *Odyssey*. Attributed to a legendary ninth-century B.C. Greek poet named Homer, these poems were the first important examples of European literature. They also became the national and much revered heroic epics of the later classical Greeks. According to Homer, both Athens and Sparta sent contingents to fight in the ten-year-long expedition. In fact, it was the kidnapping of Sparta's queen Helen by a Trojan prince that supposedly provoked the war. Whether this part of the legend is factual remains unknown. In any case, as Wood puts it:

> Troy was obviously not the only, or even the main, objective. The tradition in Homer in fact asserts that Troy was

one incident in a series of forays [raids]. . . . The Trojan story, then, takes in a long period of Mycenaean aggression in the coasts and islands of northwest [Asia Minor]. Troy was not the only place sacked, but it was the best known to the [later] Greeks, the best built and the most difficult to defeat. . . . The city was surely destroyed. . . . Troy was deliberately demolished after a bitter siege.[8]

Helen of Troy, whose abduction by Paris, a Trojan prince, supposedly sparked the Greeks' long siege of the city.

In this woodcut from thirteenth-century Sicilian poet Guido delle Colonne's Trojan History, *the Trojans prepare to drag the famous wooden horse into their city. They are unaware, of course, that Greek warriors are hiding inside the horse, ready to leap out and sack the city at the appropriate moment.*

Although most of the important Mycenaean kingdoms briefly worked together to destroy Troy, thereafter each kingdom remained separate and preoccupied with selfish interests. Even at this early date, then, the kings and peoples of Athens and Sparta, though culturally similar, were competitors for political and economic power in the Aegean sphere.

The Dark Age and the Parting of the Ways

Not long after the Trojan War, the Mycenaeans found their own Aegean supremacy shattered by the invasion of the Dorians, a nomadic warlike people who had for some time inhabited the remote and rugged lands of what is now extreme northern Greece. Beginning shortly before 1100 B.C., one by one the Mycenaean kingdoms fell before the fire and sword of the Dorian menace. Some local Greeks fled

and established new cities on the coasts and islands of Asia Minor, an area that soon became known as Greek Ionia. The Dorians conquered and absorbed most of the remaining Mycenaeans, especially in the Peloponnesus, where the main wave of Dorian invaders settled. There, the harsh Dorian military ethic that would profoundly shape the later evolution of Sparta took firm root. With the arrival of the uncultured Dorians, Greece sank into a three-hundred-year-long dark age. During these years of widespread poverty, illiteracy, and general hardship, says scholar Pierre Leveque in *The Birth of Greece*, life was "generally brutal."

It is likely that half of the population was decimated in the upheavals. The small communities that resurfaced, in many cases amid the ruins of former palaces, were primitive and isolated. . . . Each was ruled by a king, but these tribal kings were nothing like the all-powerful despots of former times. The new rulers were simply the offspring of tribal warlords who . . . claimed the best lands for their people. The king was assisted by a council composed of tribal leaders.[9]

The onset of the dark age marked the great parting of the ways for Athens and Sparta. For, in contrast to Sparta, which had been completely overrun by the invaders, Athens was the one major fortress-town the Dorians never occupied. According to historian John A. Crow, refugees fleeing the invaders

> poured [into Athens] from the surrounding country, and without forgetting its Mycenaean roots Athens grew. The light that burned on the [Athenian] Acropolis [the city's central, defensive hill] was never extinguished. Indeed, on the Greek mainland Athens was the only unbroken link between the old civilization and the new.[10]

The nature of this "new" Greek civilization was shaped in large degree by the terrain of the country, a patchwork of steep mountains, narrow valleys, and secluded offshore islands. In these sheltered environments many different societies evolved, most consisting of a rocky acropolis surrounded by a central town, itself surrounded by small villages and farmlands. Though most of these towns looked fairly similar, their inhabitants developed distinctive local customs, governments, and traditions. These city-states, which the Greeks called *poleis*, came to think of themselves as tiny separate nations. During the dark age of Greece, about which little is known, a typical polis supported no more than a few thousand residents and remained largely isolated from its neighbors.

A Liberal Melting Pot of Traditions and Ideas

The exception, once again, was Athens. For reasons that are still unknown, the peoples of the various towns of Attica decided to transfer their sovereignty, as well as their individual human and material resources, to Athens. Historian Charles Robinson Jr. comments on the uniqueness of this situation:

> The characteristic political feature of historical Greece, the city-state, was a vigorously independent community. For example, in Boeotia, the district north of Attica, there were many such city-states, and we may speak of the people as Thebans [from Thebes] and Thespians [from Thespiae] and so on, or collectively as Boeotians. But never may we speak of Atticans. The inhabitants of Eleusis, Marathon, Sunium, and the other towns of Attica were, all of them, Athenians.[11]

This display of local unity gave Athens a larger population, more land, and more resources, and therefore allowed it to recover from the negative effects of the dark age quicker than other poleis.

Thus, when prosperity returned to most of Greece by about 800 B.C.—the end of the dark age and beginning of what scholars call the Archaic Age—Athens already had a healthy head start. As Attica supported large-scale farming and enjoyed increasing foreign trade, the city of Athens grew and housed a growing class of well-to-do aristocrats, a term derived from the Greek word *aristoi*, meaning "best people." These wealthy individuals influenced the way the state and society

This view of Athens is taken from the east during the second century A.D. when Greece was part of the Roman Empire. Most of the structures built during the Periclean age were still intact at this time.

developed by investing less money in defensive walls and weapons and more in material comforts. "The Athenians," wrote the fifth-century B.C. Greek historian Thucydides, "were the first [Greeks] who laid aside arms and adopted an easier and more luxurious way of life."[12]

Because of its widespread trade relations and intellectual openness, over time Athens became a liberal melting pot of different traditions and ideas. This made it a natural breeding ground for political experimentation, including the introduction of equitable laws and democratic principles. In the first clear example of this process, the Athenians early abolished their kingship and installed a ruling council of aristocrats. This system of oligarchy, or "rule of the few," was an example

copied by most other evolving poleis across Greece.

In the sixth century B.C. Athens took more daring steps toward democracy. In 594 an aristocrat named Solon became the chief archon, or government administrator, of the city. At the time, wrote Plutarch in his *Life of Solon,* "The Athenians relapsed into their perennial squabbles about the form their government should take." Some wanted to institute democracy and others to retain oligarchy. "At this point, the most level-headed of the Athenians began to look toward Solon . . . and so finally they appealed to him to come forward and settle their differences."[13] Solon proceeded to revise the city's laws fairly, to abolish old debts so that people of all classes could have a fresh financial start, and to set up the Assembly, a group of male citizens, including poor ones, to propose new laws. As Solon described his own measures:

> To the mass of the people I gave the power they needed, neither degrading them, nor giving them too much rein: for those who already possessed great power and wealth I saw to it that their interests were not harmed. I stood guard with a broad shield before both parties and prevented either from triumphing unjustly.[14]

Athens instituted even more dramatic democratic reforms in about 507 B.C. under the politician Cleisthenes. He and his supporters greatly increased the Assembly's powers, giving every free adult male the right to speak out and vote. They also created the Council, a group of five hundred citizens chosen each year by lot, to formulate new laws and policies. The Assembly debated and voted on the Council's recommendations. In universal yearly elections, the citizens chose three archons to run the government and ten military generals, the *strategoi*, to command the army. Thus, as Athens emerged from the Archaic Age into the Classic Age, it had the world's first true working democracy. Inspired by Athens, a number of other Greek states instituted more open, liberal political procedures and institutions.

Leader of the Peloponnesus

By contrast, while many other states engaged in political experimentation and developed open attitudes, all through the Archaic Age Sparta remained a closed and rigidly conservative polis. Clinging to the militaristic traditions left behind by their Dorian forebears, the Spartans maintained what, in Greece, amounted to a politically backward and socially repressive society. Sparta retained its kings (two ruling jointly at all times), although it had a council of elders who overshadowed them in all but religious and military matters.

To the Spartans, however, military matters were supreme. Nearly every social custom, tradition, and institution was a part of or influenced by the *agoge*, a harsh and regimented military system designed to turn out strong, effective warriors. The system certainly achieved this goal. By the mid-seventh century B.C. Sparta had the most powerful and widely feared army in all of Greece.

But the cost of this power to Spartan society was great. Distrusting change, the Spartans came to avoid contact with most other poleis, which they regarded as much too liberal and unstable. In this regard they looked on Athens with particular suspicion, viewing its broadening democracy as radical and its influence on other states as dangerous. Also, for the most part the Spartans criticized as frivolous art and most literature, as well as splendid architecture and all manner of luxuries. So they discouraged these things in favor of simple necessities. To the outside world Sparta appeared not only secluded, but also small, modest, and unadorned, a look that belied its real power and influence. Thucydides put it this way:

> Suppose the city of the Spartans to be deserted and nothing left but the temples and the foundations of buildings; distant ages would be very unwilling to believe that their power was at all

equal to their fame. And yet they control two-fifths of the Peloponnesus and are acknowledged leaders of the whole, as well as of numerous allies in the rest of Greece.[15]

In fact, during the Archaic Age Sparta acquired numerous allies, some by force of arms and others through negotiation. The Spartans exerted their strongest influence over the other poleis of the Peloponnesus, all of which they virtually controlled by

about 520 B.C. These included Messenia in the southwest; Elis in the northwest; Tegea and Mantinea in the central region, known as Arcadia; Argos in the northeastern sector, a peninsula commonly called the Argolid; and Corinth, located in a strategic position on the Isthmus of Corinth, the strip of land connecting the Peloponnesus to the rest of Greece. Corinth was also an important commercial center, as Thucydides pointed out in his introduction to *The Peloponnesian Wars:*

The dromos, *or public walkway, in ancient Sparta. Here, the Spartans staged athletic contests, military training and drills, and other important communal activities.*

"A Magnificent and Terrible Sight"

In the Life of Lycurgus, *part of his collection of biographies titled* Lives of the Noble Grecians and Romans, *the Greek/Roman historian Plutarch described the formidable Spartan army in action. This excerpt describes the ceremonial sendoff of troops to battle.*

"When their army was drawn up in battle array, and the enemy near, the king sacrificed a goat, commanded the soldiers to set their garlands upon their heads, and the pipers to play the tune of the hymn to Castor [a mortal son of the god Zeus], and himself began [singing] the paean [battle hymn] of advance. It was at once a magnificent and terrible sight to see them march on to the tune of their flutes, without any disorder in their ranks, any discomposure [doubt] in their minds, or change in their expressions, calmly and cheerfully moving with the music to the deadly fight. Men, in this temper, were not likely to be possessed with fear . . . but with the deliberate valor of hope and assurance, as if some divinity were attending and conducting them. . . . After they had routed [defeated] an enemy, they pursued him till they were well assured of the victory, and then they sounded a retreat, thinking it mean and unworthy of a Greek people to cut men to pieces, who had given up and abandoned all resistance."

Corinth, being seated on the isthmus, was naturally always a center of commerce; for the Greeks inside and outside the Peloponnesus in the old days, when they communicated chiefly by land, had to pass through her territory in order to reach one another. Her wealth too was a source of power, as the ancient poets have made plain, who speak of "Corinth the rich." When navigation grew more common, the Corinthians, having acquired a fleet, were able to put down piracy; they offered a market both by sea and land, and the power of their city increased with the revenues.[16]

Athens Passes the Test

Sparta's dominance over Corinth and the other Peloponnesian poleis signaled the emergence of a solid Spartan federation to challenge the growing power and influence of Athens. In the sixth century B.C., as the Archaic Age was drawing to a close, Athens made some initial, and in the eyes of many other Greeks ominous, steps toward what would later become a full-fledged empire. It seized the island of Salamis, located just off Attica's western shore, and also a strip of land on the western shore of Euboea, the large island lying

The two soldiers at left are fully armed hoplites, or heavy infantry, having shields, cuirasses (breastplates), and greaves (leg protectors); the lightly armed figure at right is an ekdromos, *or "outside runner," trained to chase down and kill enemy spear-throwers.*

along Attica's northern coast. In addition, the Athenians secured control of the Thracian Chersonese, the peninsula bordering the Hellespont, the narrow water channel separating Europe from Asia Minor and leading into the Black Sea. To support its large and still growing population, Athens needed grain from the fertile lands bordering that sea. Control of the Chersonese ensured that its life-giving grain connection would remain intact.

Athens also sought allies from its neighboring region of Boeotia. But at first most of the Boeotian poleis, among them Thebes, Thespiae, Phocis, Tanagra, and Coronea, were worried about Athenian expansion and therefore reluctant to ally themselves to Athens. These political entities formed a Boeotian federation headed by the most powerful member, Thebes. But the tiny Boeotian polis of Plataea, located on the northwestern border of Attica, refused to join the others. In 506 B.C., when Thebes threatened the use of military force, the Plataeans appealed to

Athens for help. Eager to demonstrate the strength of their new democracy, the Athenians took upon themselves the role of Greece's champion of freedom and justice and quickly marched to Plataea's rescue. An Athenian force defeated the Theban army in a small but decisive battle in southern Boeotia.

In their victory, the Athenians demonstrated their skill in hoplite warfare, which had been developing in Greece for about three centuries and at which the Spartans were the acknowledged masters. A Greek hoplite was a heavily armored infantry soldier who carried a round shield called a *hoplon*, a six-foot-long spear, and a short sword. Hoplites fought in a special and very lethal formation known as a phalanx, described here by military historian Peter Connolly:

The phalanx was a long block of soldiers several ranks deep. There were usually eight ranks, but there could be as few as four, or many more than eight. The phalanx was organized in files (lines from front to back) so that when a man fell his place was taken by the man [in the file] behind. . . . This way of fighting was made possible by a . . . round shield, held across the chest [which] covered a warrior from chin to knees. When the phalanx was in close [tightly packed] order, the shield was wide enough to protect the unguarded side of the man on the left.[17]

Usually, the hoplites marched at the enemy in this regimented phalanx formation. While the men in the front rank jabbed their spears at the enemy, those in the rear ranks pushed at the backs of their comrades, giving the whole formation a huge and deadly forward momentum.

The defeat of Thebes at the hands of the Athenian phalanx alarmed many Greeks, especially the Spartans, who were already deeply concerned about recent democratic reforms in Athens. Most Peloponnesians and Boeotians concluded that Athens's aggressive political and military policies needed to be thwarted. To that end, Sparta gathered a large force of Peloponnesian hoplites and marched north, while the Thebans rallied allies from among their fellow Boeotians. The plan was to assail Attica from both sides and whip Athens into submission. But the scheme failed miserably. According to classical historian J. B. Bury:

> The Peloponnesian host under the two [Spartan] kings, Cleomenes and Demaratus, passed the isthmus [of Corinth] and occupied Eleusis; and the Athenians marched to the Eleusian plain [to meet the foe]. But the peril on this side [of Attica] passed

away without a blow. The Corinthians, on second thoughts, disapproved of the expedition, as unjust, and returned to Corinth. . . . This action of the Corinthians discouraged the whole army, and the situation was aggravated by . . . discord between the Spartan leaders. In the end the army broke up, and there was nothing left for Cleomenes but to return home.[18]

The Athenian phalanx then proceeded north and delivered the Thebans another and even more crushing defeat.

Athens's new democracy had passed its first supreme survival test against formidable odds. But it had done so at the expense of the proud Spartans and Thebans, and this humiliation would have important consequences later. For their loss of face, both Sparta and Thebes would carry into the new century's political and military arena a deep-seated grudge against the Athenians. The episode foreshadowed, as well, the deadly mode of warfare to come—armed confrontation between entire leagues of Greek poleis.

Victory over Persia

However, at the start of the fifth century B.C. the inevitable clash of the city-states was unexpectedly postponed. This surprising break was due to two successive invasions of Greece by Persia, a far-flung and mighty empire centered near the Persian Gulf in what is now Iran. In 499 B.C., Miletus and several other Greek Ionian cities in Asia Minor rebelled against the Persians, who had subjugated them several decades earlier. Athens, which had kept close ties with the Ionians since Mycenaean times, sent ships and men to help the rebels. Together, the Athenians and Ionians burned Sardis, the capital of Persia's province in Asia Minor.

Seeking revenge against Athens and desiring to initiate a conquest of Europe at the same time, the Persian king, Darius, sent a force of some sixty thousand men across the Aegean. But in 490 B.C., before the Persians could acquire a foothold on the Greek mainland, they were soundly defeated by the Athenians, aided by a small band of Plataeans, on the plain of Marathon in northern Attica. The fifth-century B.C. Greek historian Herodotus recorded the reaction of Darius to the news of the Battle of Marathon:

His anger against Athens, already great enough on account of the as-

sault on Sardis, was even greater, and he was more determined than ever to make war on Greece. Without loss of time he dispatched couriers to the various states under his dominion with orders to raise an army much larger than before; and also warships, transports, horses, and grain.[19]

Numerous delays, including the death of Darius, put off the invasion for ten years. When the new Persian king, Xerxes, finally launched an attack in 480 B.C., he used at least eight hundred ships and over two hundred thousand soldiers. The Greek poleis, none of which could field armies larger than a few thousand men, appeared doomed. However, in a remarkable display of unity, fighting skill, and sheer courage, the Greeks handed the in-

The Athenians and Plataeans drive the Persians to their ships in the climax of the Battle of Marathon. Greatly outnumbered, the Greeks won a decisive victory.

Athenian crowds triumphantly celebrate on the beaches after the Greeks' crushing defeat of the Persian fleet in the Bay of Salamis.

vaders a series of decisive and embarrassing defeats. After the Greek victories at Salamis in 480 and Plataea in 479, the Persians retreated to Asia, leaving the triumphant Greeks with profound new feelings of personal strength and achievement. Writes John Crow:

> After the defeat of the Persians, the Greek spirit rose to new heights. . . . A dynamic spirit flooded all Greece. There was nothing that the Greeks could not accomplish [they believed] if they set their minds to it. . . . What, then, would the Greeks do next? They had boundless energy and the field was open before them. The answer, oversimplified no doubt, is that they created the world's greatest civilization.[20]

In this way, then, the victory over Persia provided much of the confidence that motivated the grand achievements of the subsequent Fifty Years and golden age of Athens.

Yet the joyous and optimistic opening of the new age was tempered by the sober political realities of the day. Sparta and Athens had emerged as the two leading states in Greece. With the Persian menace out of the way, their temporary unity dissolved and the rivalry between their two camps was rekindled. As Thucydides pointed out, "The barbarians [Persians] were repelled by a common effort; but soon the Greeks . . . took different sides and became the allies of the Athenians or of the Spartans, for there were now two leading powers, the one strong by land and the other by sea."[21] Each side was determined to make itself the *single* leading power in Greece. And so began what would prove one of the most glorious, and at the same time most tragic, periods in human history.

2 From Alliance to Empire: The Aegean Becomes an Athenian Lake

As the famed Fifty Years began in the wake of the Greek victory over Persia, Pericles, the man who would come to dominate the politics of the age, was perhaps seventeen years old. Still a year shy of the legal age necessary for attending meetings of the Assembly, he had not yet entered the arena of Athenian politics. Therefore, the first phase of the *Pentekontaetia*, lasting from about 478 to 461 B.C., was dominated and driven by other powerful men. Among the most important of these were Themistocles, the victor of the sea battle of Salamis, whose foresight in building a powerful navy had saved Greece from Persian subjugation; the able general and politician Cimon, son of Miltiades, the general who had led the successful Athenian phalanx at Marathon; and Ephialtes, Pericles' political mentor, a staunch democrat who vigorously promoted government reforms.

The School of Danger

It was no coincidence that these and most of the other important leaders who spearheaded Greek politics at the time were Athenians. To be sure, Sparta had emerged from the Persian wars with power and influence equal to that of Athens. But Spartan leaders, including Pausanias, victor over the Persians at Plataea, were much less effective as politicians and diplomats than they had been as military commanders. Pausanias was only one of several Spartan leaders of the period who fell from power and embarrassed their countrymen by drawing accusations of political corruption.

Another factor that kept Sparta from initiating important Greek policy was that it maintained its traditional approach to relations with other poleis. While the Athenians were outgoing, forceful, and ambitious in their relations with neighbors, the Spartans were aloof, reluctant to stray far from home, and notoriously cautious and slow to act. Thus, in the realm of international politics, Athens acted boldly, while Sparta tended to do nothing, or to *re*act. And when the Spartans did react, they employed mainly the tool they knew best—the power of their renowned and deadly phalanx. The result was that after the Persian wars, as Thucydides put it, "the Spartans and the Athenians were perpetually fighting or making peace, either with one another or with their own rebellious allies; thus they attained military efficiency and learned experience in the school of danger."[22]

Though Sparta was notoriously cautious and slow to act, when it did so its impact was significant, for its warriors, pictured here, were the most skilled and feared in all Greece.

For the Athenians, that perpetual school of danger acted as a kind of stimulant. Taking an offensive rather than defensive posture, they were ever on the move, seeking always to expand their interests and improve themselves. Their intrepid spirit and vigorous foreign policy, combined with their unusually open society, one that encouraged experiment and personal expression, set the tone for their phenomenal cultural ascendancy in the Fifty Years. Comments John Crow:

> Today when we think of the heritage of Greece we think of Athens, and it is fitting that we should. . . . In Greece there was only one Athens. Her leadership in the wars with Persia and her subsequent rivalry with Sparta helped

to create the dynamic tension out of which her great culture emerged.[23]

The Delian League

Following the expulsion of the Persians from the Aegean sphere, Athens wasted no time in attempting to assert its influence and leadership over other Greek states. In the minds of most Greeks, the Persians, though defeated, continued to pose a serious threat. The Persian empire was still vast and strong and might at any time launch a new invasion of Ionia or even the Greek mainland. Greek unity had worked against the Persians once, and many Greek leaders supported some form of continuation of that unity. The Athenians quickly offered to assume leadership of a new anti-Persian alliance. "Their eagerness is not difficult to understand," explains historian Donald Kagan:

> The Aegean and its borders were outside the normal sphere of Sparta's interest, and involvement in that region was as dangerous to Sparta as it was inviting. For Athens the situation was quite different. Recent events had shown that in the case of Persian attack Athens was vulnerable. The Athenian economy was increasingly dependent upon trade, a large part of it in the Aegean and in the Hellespontine region [gateway to the Black Sea grain route]. . . . She could not allow the Hellespont and northern Aegean to remain . . . under threat of Persian control. Athens, moreover, felt an emotional attachment to the Ionians, and their abandonment to Persian rule would have been difficult for Athenian politicians to justify.[24]

Other Greek states had their own reasons for an alliance, but common to all were the desires to seek protection from and revenge against the Persian empire. With these officially stated goals, in the winter of 478–477 B.C. the Athenians presided over a large meeting of delegates from over 150 Ionian, island, and mainland poleis. Because the congress took place on the small island of Delos, located in the strategic center of the Aegean, the alliance became commonly known as the Delian League. However, its official name, which translates roughly as "The Athenians and Their Allies," was more reflective of the organization's true nature. Although it was supposed to be an alliance of equals, Athens made no bones about dominating the body's affairs and policies from the start. "The Athenians," wrote Thucydides, "fixed [dictated] which of the cities should supply money and which ships for the war against the barbarians."[25]

Swearing an Oath to Remain Forever United

For the poleis expected to contribute money, the total sum of individual fees in the first year was 460 talents, more than five thousand times the amount an average Greek worker earned annually. At first the league money was kept in a treasury on Delos, but Athenian officials always collected and transported it. Athens exerted its control even more blatantly by insisting that many of the member states contribute ships to the league navy. Here, selfish motives were not hard to discern. Athenian admirals commanded these ships, which meant that the league's fleet was at Athens's disposal. In addition, Athens supplied a majority of the oarsmen and sailors for the league ships, thereby helping substantially to relieve the city's unemployment. Indeed, it was partly because of Athens's manipulation of the league that Sparta refused to join and made sure that its own allies did not do so. Many Spartans worried that Athens might eventually use the Delian alliance as a tool to oppose the Peloponnesian League, a fear that would turn out to be well founded.

By contrast, the other members of the Delian League seemed unbothered by the domination of Athens. It seemed only natural that the largest and, besides Sparta, the most powerful polis in Greece would assume a clear leadership role. And the member states, eager to begin an anti-Persian campaign, realized that strong central military leadership was essential to success. In a spirit of comradeship, then, the league delegates threw swords into the Aegean waters and swore an oath to remain united until these weapons floated

to the surface. And then they swung into action. First, they swept through the Aegean, rooting out and punishing Greeks who had aided the enemy during the Persian wars. Next, they launched an offensive against numerous Persian cities in Asia Minor, a campaign they would continue to wage almost ceaselessly for the next several years.

Transforming the Delian League

The Delian League had several advantages over the Spartan-led Peloponnesian League. For one, the Athenian-led alliance could and did act more swiftly and decisively. As classical scholar Donald Kagan explains in this excerpt from The Outbreak of the Peloponnesian War, *the Delian League also had sounder financial arrangements, which ultimately facilitated its transformation into an Athenian empire.*

"Up to the conflict with Athens the Spartan alliance had little need for money. Campaigns were almost always on land, and the Spartans demanded from their allies only that they send the required military contingents. . . . The Delian League, on the contrary, was chiefly a naval confederation whose purposes required that it maintain a fleet . . . for an indefinite period. This was a costly undertaking and demanded a well-organized system for regular payments into the league treasury. Athens was given the responsibility of making the assessment and of collecting the money. . . . Heaviest of all [among the league members] was the burden borne by Athens, which not only provided leadership but the largest fleet as well, which she manned and maintained. No doubt booty collected from the Persians was expected to, and did, meet some of the cost, but the expenditure of [Athenian] time, effort, and lives was not insignificant. . . . Of course, as the allies shrank from responsibility, the Athenians accepted more of it. This centralizing tendency helped make the league more effective against external enemies, but it led to a gradual but decisive change in the nature of the organization. By the time of the Peloponnesian War Athenian statesmen were willing to admit that the Delian League had become an empire and that Athens ruled it as a tyrant."

The Rise of Cimon

The league's supreme military commander was Cimon, a wealthy, personable, and popular young Athenian aristocrat. According to Plutarch, the elements of his character were

> noble and deserve our admiration. He was as brave as Miltiades [his father] and as intelligent as Themistocles [known for his shrewdness], and he is generally admitted to have been a juster man than either. In all qualities which war demands he was fully their equal, and in statesmanship he showed himself immeasurably their superior, even when he was quite young and inexperienced in military matters. . . . His physical appearance was imposing, too . . . for he was tall with a thick and curly head of hair.[26]

Cimon's political leanings were pro-Spartan. He and his supporters believed that Athens and Sparta should try to maintain the unity they had achieved during the Persian wars and work together for the benefit of all Greeks. Since keeping up at least cordial relations with Sparta allowed Athens to go about its business unhindered by the Peloponnesians, Cimon's ideas enjoyed considerable support. As Plutarch put it:

> At first the Athenians were well pleased . . . since the goodwill the Spartans showed them was very much to their advantage. So in the early days of their empire, and while they were still engaged in building alliances, they welcomed the honors and favors that were shown to Cimon, since it was

through him, in fact, that most of their negotiations with other Greek states were carried on. . . . But afterwards, when their power had grown and they saw that Cimon was wholeheartedly attached to the Spartans, they resented this, not least because of his tendency to sing the praises of Sparta to the Athenians whenever he had occasion to reproach [scold] them or spur them on.[27]

For a while, Cimon's chief political opponent was Themistocles, who was notoriously anti-Spartan. While Cimon was busy commanding the Delian League's forces, Themistocles dominated the political scene back in Athens and pursued policies that repeatedly infuriated Sparta. For example, Themistocles ordered the construction of huge defensive walls around

The pro-Spartan policies of the personable general and politician Cimon at first had widespread support in Athens.

Winning the Hearts of His Countrymen

In his Life of Cimon, *Plutarch listed some of the reasons for Cimon's extraordinary and long-lived popularity as an Athenian general and politician.*

"He quickly won not only the praise but also the hearts of his countrymen. . . . What was it, then, in Cimon's achievements which gave such intense pleasure to the people? The answer is probably that under their other generals they had merely been defending themselves against attack and fighting for self-preservation, whereas under Cimon they had the opportunity to carry the [Persian] war into their enemies' country and ravage it, and besides this they won new territory which they could colonize. . . . Cimon was already a rich man, and so he saw to it that the money which he . . . won honorably from the enemy in his campaigns was spent even more honorably on his fellow-citizens. He had all the fences on the fields taken down, so that not only poor Athenians but even strangers could help themselves freely to whatever fruit was in season. He also provided a dinner at his house every day, a simple meal but enough for large numbers. Any poor man who wished could come to him for this. . . . He always went about attended by a number of young men fitted out with good new clothes, each of whom was ready, if Cimon met some elderly and poorly dressed citizen, to change clothes with him. . . . The same attendants also carried with them plenty of ready money, and would go up to . . . the poor in the marketplace and quietly slip some small change into their hands."

both Athens and its port town of Piraeus. Seeing the building of such fortifications as an unfriendly and warlike move and as part of an ominous trend toward expansionism, the Spartans objected. Themistocles noted the objection and curtly rebuffed it.

But Themistocles was never able to garner the public popularity and political support that Cimon enjoyed. Cimon exploited this situation and eventually prevailed over his rival. In 472 B.C., undoubtedly urged on by Spartan leaders, Cimon's supporters accused Themistocles of taking bribes, a charge that stuck despite the absence of clear supporting evidence. Themistocles then underwent ostracism, a democratic process the Athenians had instituted the decade before. The citizenry met periodically and cast votes calling for the banishment from Attica of a public official. Any official was "eligible" for this negative election, and the period of banishment, or ostracism, was ten years. Themistocles received the most negative votes in 472 and accordingly went into exile, leaving Cimon the most powerful figure in Athens.

"I Will Obey the People of Athens"

Riding a wave of popular support, Cimon led the forces of Athens and its league allies to victory after victory over the Persians. These campaigns culminated in 469 B.C. in a large battle fought both on land and at sea near the mouth of the Eurymedon River on the southern coast of Asia Minor. According to Victor Ehrenberg:

It was a decisive event, especially when soon afterwards Xerxes [the Persian king] was murdered by his brother and successor Artaxerxes, who had then to quell various revolts within the Persian empire. The Greeks rightly celebrated the battle of Eurymedon as one of their outstanding victories. . . . Cimon's success . . . [meant that]

These surviving ostracism ballots, shards of pottery called ostrakons, *bear the names of the politicians (top to bottom) Themistocles, Pericles, Aristides, Allixenos, and Cimon.*

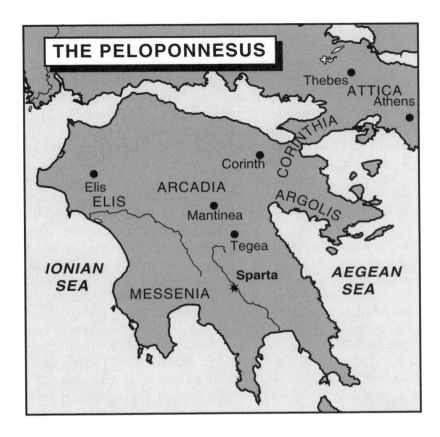

THE PELOPONNESUS

Greek rule over the Aegean was now uncontested.[28]

But the Aegean was already becoming less a Greek waterway and more an Athenian lake. While employing the league's power to thwart the Persians, Cimon began asserting Athens's power over its own allies. Confirming Sparta's earlier fears, Athens became increasingly imperialistic and steadily transformed the Delian League into its own empire. To expand their wealth, influence, and prestige, the Athenians used the alliance's powerful naval forces to intimidate and control smaller league members. "The Athenians were exacting and oppressive," recorded Thucydides, "using coercive measures

against men who were neither accustomed nor willing to [do what Athens required of them]."[29]

The first league member to experience such coercive measures was Naxos, an island situated not far to the southeast of Delos. In 469, shortly after the Battle of Eurymedon, Naxos decided that the Persian threat had been eliminated. So it withdrew from the league, intending to use its ships to serve its own interests rather than those of Athens. Though according to the original league charter the Naxians had every right to resign from the organization, Cimon saw it differently. Treating the Naxians as rebellious Athenian subjects, he attacked them, destroyed their fortifications, and confiscated their fleet. Thereafter Naxos had to pay yearly tribute directly to Athens as a symbol of subservience. The inhabitants of the island polis of Thasos, located at the northern edge of the Aegean, suffered a similar fate when they rebelled against Athenian overlordship in 465 B.C. Gone was the spirit of brotherhood that had marked the league's noble beginnings. Gone too was the original oath of unity, and in its place the Athenians forced the members to swear a new oath:

> I will not revolt from the people of Athens by any manner or means, in word or in deed, nor will I obey anyone else who is in rebellion; and if anyone rebels I will denounce him to the Athenians; and I will pay the tribute which I persuade the Athenians to assess, and I will be an ally to the Athenian people as best I can and as justly as I can, and I will help and defend the people of Athens, if someone harms the people of Athens, and I will obey the people of Athens.[30]

Through intimidation and naked force when necessary, Athens swiftly expanded its empire until it encompassed over two hundred city-states in the Aegean region and beyond.

Sparta's Troubles

Not surprisingly, Sparta grew increasingly alarmed at this display of Athenian imperialism, seeing the new Athenian empire as a dangerous menace that upset the balance of power in Greece. To the Spartans, there seemed no limit to Athenian arro-

gance and greed for power and wealth. Fear and envy of Athens also grew strong in Corinth, Sparta's ally. Their markets steadily shrinking as a result of Athens's growing stranglehold on Aegean trade and shipping, the Corinthians pleaded with the Spartans to act.

The Spartans certainly wanted to clip Athens's wings, especially after the cruel subjugation and punishment of Naxos and Thasos. During these opening years of the *Pentekontaetia*, however, Sparta was beset by one serious local crisis after another and thus unable to commit its energy and resources outside the Peloponnesus. The prestige lost in the wake of the corruption charges against Pausanias in the mid-470s B.C. proved only the beginning. Soon afterward, several members of the Peloponnesian League, openly defying Sparta, dismantled their Spartan-approved oligarchies. First Argos, and then Elis, Mantinea, and Tegea, apparently inspired by the Athenian model, began setting up their own democracies. Its leadership of the Peloponnesus threatened, in 473 Sparta sent its phalanx into Arcadia and defeated troops from Argos and the other upstart poleis. But some, especially the Tegeans, continued to resist. Not until it had won another decisive hoplite battle in Arcadia in 469 did Sparta regain its undisputed mastery of the Peloponnesus.

Sparta's troubles were far from over, however. In 464, its powerful phalanx was helpless against a more formidable natural disaster. Plutarch recorded that

> the country suffered the most terrible earthquake in all its history. The earth opened in many places, several of the peaks of Mt. Taygetos [on Sparta's western border] were torn away and the

A view of ancient Sparta shows the Eurotas River flowing in the foreground and the peaks of Mount Taygetos rising in the distance.

whole city of Sparta was destroyed, with the exception of five houses. Archidamus [one of Sparta's kings] at once understood that the immediate disaster harbored yet another for the state.[31]

The new disaster that Archidamus feared was an uprising of the Spartan serfs, a class of poor and oppressed agricultural workers known as helots. Though the helots outnumbered Spartan citizens at least ten to one, they normally were kept well in line through the use of armed guards and strict, often brutal punitive measures. With the Spartan ruling class crippled by the quake, however, the helots took advantage of what they saw as their only chance for freedom. The rebellion was swift and widespread, and it plunged Sparta further into chaos. Eventually, though, the tough and resilient Spartans were able to regroup and deploy their crack troops; the rebels, of course, no longer had a chance. Still, a large group of helots managed to resist the effects of a savage siege of their mountain stronghold,

Many Athenians, including Ephialtes and Pericles, hoped to abolish the Areopagus, Greece's ancient oligarchic council, to strengthen the democracy.

and it took the Spartans almost five years to completely stamp out the rebellion.

The Areopagus

As it happened, the early stages of the helot rebellion also worsened relations between Sparta and Athens and finally brought about Cimon's downfall. Opposition in Athens to Cimon's pro-Spartan stance had been growing for some time, partly because of Sparta's suppression of the fledgling democracies in the Argolid and Arcadia. The politician Ephialtes, aided by his able assistant, young Pericles, also attacked Cimon by opposing the Areopagus. This ancient oligarchic council, made up of former archons who served for life instead of running for re-election, exerted considerable influence over the Assembly and other democratic institutions. Seeing it as the last major

Aristides the Just

In his Life of Aristides, *Plutarch explained how the procedure of ostracism worked. He also passed on a famous tale about the Athenian leader Aristides, known as "the Just," whose renowned honesty and integrity were illuminated in this discouraging encounter.*

"The procedure, to give a general account of it, was as follows. Each voter took an *ostrakon*, or piece of earthenware, wrote on it the name of the citizen he wished to be banished and carried it to a part of the market-place which was fenced off. . . . Then the archons first counted the total number of votes cast, for if there were less than six thousand, the ostracism was void. After this they sorted the votes and the man who had the most recorded against his name was proclaimed to be exiled for ten years, with the right, however, to receive the income from his estate. The story goes that [when Aristides was being ostracized], while the votes were being written down, an illiterate and uncouth rustic [country bumpkin] handed his piece of earthenware to Aristides and asked him to write the name Aristides on it. The latter was astonished and asked the man what harm Aristides had ever done him. 'None whatever,' was the reply, 'I do not even know the fellow, but I am sick of hearing him called The Just everywhere!' When he heard this, Aristides said nothing, but wrote his name on the *ostrakon* and handed it back."

Aristides, known for his honesty and integrity, served as one of Athens's ten generals at the Battle of Marathon and later led its forces at the Battle of Plataea, in which the Greeks annihilated the Persian army.

impediment to complete democracy in Athens, Ephialtes, Pericles, and other democrats wanted to abolish it. But Cimon stood in their way. Because the Areopagus usually backed the interests of the wealthy old guard of aristocrats, Cimon supported it, and as long as he was popular, it was safe.

Cimon's Undoing

But in 462 B.C. the desperate Spartans, their hands full trying to rebuild their shattered city and fight the helots at the same time, swallowed their pride and asked the Athenians for help. The debate in Athens over whether to send such aid was loud and bitter. According to Plutarch in his *Life of Cimon*:

> Ephialtes opposed the request and pleaded with the Athenians not to attempt to rescue or restore a city which was their rival but rather to let Sparta's pride be trampled underfoot. Cimon, on the other hand, put Sparta's interests before his own country's . . . and persuaded the Athenians to send a large force of hoplites to her aid.[32]

This turned out to be Cimon's undoing. The Athenian hoplites, most of them already unhappy about their assignment, found a rude rebuff awaiting them in Sparta. As Donald Kagan puts it, they "had not been on the scene long before the Spartans sharply changed their policy. For no apparent reason they . . . sent them [the Athenians] home on the grounds that they no longer needed them."[33] This insult enraged Athenians of all classes, who, incited by the rousing speeches of Ephialtes and Pericles, blamed Cimon. The democrats arranged for an ostracism vote early in 461, and when the ballots were counted, Cimon was banished, leaving Ephialtes the most powerful leader in Athens.

With Cimon out of the way, Ephialtes wasted no time in assaulting the Areopagus, quickly reducing its powers solely to hearing and judging murder cases. But the new democratic leader was unable to follow through with further reforms. Later that year he was assassinated, an unusual occurrence in Athens. The probable instigators were disgruntled aristocrats, unhappy about the ostracism of Cimon and the great reduction in the power of the Areopagus. In his mentor's stead, Pericles, now about thirty-four, assumed leadership of the democrats and, in effect, of the Athenian state. No one, including Pericles himself, could have guessed at that moment that he would remain in power for more than thirty years, during which he would lead Athens to glories that would be remembered for all time.

3 An Amazing Energy: Athens's Struggle to Maintain Supremacy

A new phase of the Fifty Years began when Pericles came to power in Athens in 461 B.C. Technically, he was but one of the ten annually elected *strategoi*, who commanded the military forces and carried out the foreign policies of the people. And initially, he was certainly not the most experienced and influential *strategos*. Older generals, including Myronides, Leocrates, and Tolmides, each probably held more individual authority in the Assembly.

But Pericles was young, energetic, popular, and an extraordinarily talented public speaker. He was also the leader and spokesman of the democratic faction in Athens, in the same way that the president of the United States is the head of his own political party. For these reasons, the nine colleagues of Pericles often deferred to his judgment or allowed him to speak for them. During the next decade, that of the turbulent 450s B.C., Pericles managed to

This drawing depicts Pericles making a speech to an Athenian crowd. It was his skill and power as an orator, along with his enthusiasm and shrewdness as a politician, that made him widely popular.

The Classical Greek Trireme

The main instrument of Athens's power in the Periclean age was its navy, composed mainly of vessels called triremes, which had become the standard warships of the Mediterranean by the end of the sixth century B.C. *This description of the classical Greek trireme is from* The Greek Armies *by historian Peter Connolly.*

"There is still a great deal of controversy surrounding the trireme but certain factors are clear. It was rowed at three levels with one man at each oar. . . . We learn from Athenian naval records that these oars were between 4 and 4.5 meters [about 14 feet] long. Athenian ship sheds at Piraeus have been excavated. These give maximum dimensions for the ships, that is, 37 meters [about 120 feet] long, 3 meters [ten feet] wide at the bottom, increasing to about 6 meters at outrigger level. According to Athenian records there were 27 rowers [on] each side at the lowest level. . . . There were 27 rowers in the second bank. The top bank . . . [had] 31 rowers on each side. . . . The crew of a trireme was 200 of whom 170 were rowers. These were drawn from the lower classes. They were not slaves. . . . The ship was commanded by a *trierarch* who was appointed by the general. The main weapon was the bronze-plated ram at the front. . . . To estimate a trireme's greatest speed is impossible . . . [but it was] possibly 12 to 15 kilometers [about 9 miles] per hour."

retain his important position by repeatedly winning reelection to high office. By steadily enhancing his political reputation and gathering a wide array of supporters, he slowly but surely became the most important and powerful leader in Athens and, indeed, in all of Greece.

During this early stage of his career, Pericles was constantly busy, perpetually involved in one aspect or another of Athens's wide-ranging foreign affairs and activities. The vibrant, enthusiastic, and ambitious Athenians became like a whirlwind spinning outward from the heart of the Greek world. They eagerly involved themselves in projects that would have

been too enormous for most other poleis even to consider. One of these enterprises, of course, was the huge job of managing Athens's swiftly expanding maritime empire. On top of that, in the 450s Athens launched a massive military expedition to a faraway land and engaged in costly ongoing military skirmishes with Sparta and other members of the Peloponnesian League. These many bold offensives drove the whole Greek world in new directions. The old, traditional, and fairly stable political landscape suddenly began to give way to a new, unfamiliar, and decidedly more dangerous one. For this reason, the decade of the 450s was, in the words of classical scholar Peter Levi, "the hinge of the century."[34]

But in creating this brave new Greek world, the Athenians were, in a sense, sealing their own fate. One of Sparta's problems had always been its tendency to do too little too slowly. In contrast, Athens now severely overextended itself, wasting many of its huge human and material resources in an attempt to achieve too much too fast. As Levi puts it:

> The Athenians, driven on by an amazing energy, were asserting a supremacy that no one city could sustain, and even though the sea was theirs, with its commerce, the mines and the green riches of the earth, they could no more finally dominate the eastern Mediterranean than the Spartans could.[35]

Indeed, Athens's attempt to carry too large a load would have grave consequences later, both for itself and for the entire Greek world.

The Ambitious Athenians

A substantial portion of Athens's ambitious load, of course, was its management of the many and far-flung members of the Delian League. Pericles had disagreed with Cimon on many issues, but not about their city's control of the league. Realizing that such control guaranteed Athens expanding trade, inflowing wealth, and increased power and prestige, Pericles and his supporters continued to affirm Athenian supremacy. The realization that their allies were steadily becoming their subjects did not seem to bother Athenian leaders. The general attitude in Athens was that the city had not become the leader of the league by accident. Just as its patron goddess, Athena, had guided it to victory at Marathon and Salamis, the gods now ordained that Greece's savior also become its lord. In this view, guiding the affairs of the Greek world was Athens's ultimate and sacred destiny.

Therefore, Athenian leaders thought nothing of using any means necessary, including threats and physical coercion, to enforce their will. Of course, the key to such enforcement was overwhelming power. So Pericles and his fellow *strategoi* were careful to maintain a large and well-equipped fleet, just as Themistocles and Cimon had done. Historian Russell Meiggs explains in *The Athenian Empire:*

> The foundation of Athens' power was her fleet. The Delian League was composed almost entirely of islands and coastal cities and could be controlled only by a powerful fleet. . . . Athens' fleet was strong enough to face the combined fleets of the Aegean. . . . The knowledge that Athenian triremes might appear at any moment in [a] harbor was a deterrent to anti-Athenian elements. . . . The main function of the fleet in peacetime was to act as a police force. Each year . . . patrols were sent out. They showed the Athenian flag, gave confidence to Athens' friends, and kept the seas clear of pirates.[36]

While they were regulating and patrolling the whole Aegean, the Athenians embarked on a new and equally ambitious enterprise. In 460 B.C., Inaros, king of Lybia, a kingdom on Egypt's western border, initiated an Egyptian rebellion against the Persians, who had conquered Egypt nearly seventy years before. Inaros realized that to be successful he would need help, and it seemed logical to call on people who hated the Persians as much as he did. At the time, a Delian League fleet was fighting the Persians in Cyprus, the large island off the southern coast of Asia Minor. Inaros invited the Athenians to take part in the revolt and they accepted, immediately diverting most of the Cyprus fleet—perhaps two hundred or more ships loaded with hoplites and supplies, to the Nile Delta. For Athenian leaders, says J. B. Bury,

The invitation of Inaros was most alluring. It meant that, if Athens delivered Egypt from Persian rule, she would secure the chief control of the foreign trade with the Nile valley and be able to establish a naval station on the coast; by one stroke she would far outstrip all the rival merchant cities of

Greece. . . . But when the [naval] squadron passed over to Egypt, it entered a new sphere and undertook a new kind of work. The Egyptian expedition was an attempt to carry the struggle with Persia into another stage—a stage in which Greece was the aggressor and the invader.[37]

To the delight of Athens's leaders, the initial phase of the Egyptian expedition was very successful. The Greek hoplites joined forces with Inaros's troops, swept up the Nile to the city of Memphis, and wrested it from the Persians. The victors viewed this win as the beginning of the end of Persian domination of Egypt. They had no way of knowing how determined King Artaxerxes was to hold onto that land, or the size of the forces the Persian ruler would soon marshall to retain it.

Sparta: An Ominous Specter

While becoming involved in the troubles of distant Egypt, Athens took on heavy liabilities on still another front, this one the largest and potentially the most dangerous to its immediate security. Athenian-Spartan relations had been deteriorating for years. Sparta, already worried about Athenian expansionism, became particularly alarmed at the demise of Cimon, who had been sympathetic to its interests, and the corresponding ascendancy of the Athenian democrats. At first, the Spartans were too preoccupied with internal problems to deal with the threat posed by Athens. But by the early 450s B.C. they had recovered sufficiently from their troubles to focus on the need to contain Athenian imperialism.

Athenian Expeditions

THRACE
ASIA MINOR
GREECE
Crete
Cyprus
Nile Delta
LYBIA
Memphis
Nile R.
EGYPT

■ Persian Empire
✕ Athenian/Persian Battle Sites

Persia's King Artaxerxes I, successor to Xerxes, was determined to dislodge the Athenians from Egypt, an important part of his empire.

A revitalized Sparta was an ominous specter that Athens could not afford to ignore. Though the Spartans had no navy, their land troops were still by far the best in Greece. And while Sparta could not match the vast financial and material resources of Athens and the Delian League, its phalanx was relatively cheap and easy to maintain. Meiggs points out:

It was possible for the Spartans to fight a long war with very limited financial resources, because they were a land power and were trying to fight the war by land. Hoplites had to be fed on campaigns and Sparta's allies had to be paid, but an army could partly support itself on its ravaging [of the enemy's countryside] and normally campaigns were short. Fleets [like those of Athens] were very much more expensive.[38]

Sparta also had the advantage of its allies, both inside and outside the Peloponnesus, who helped even the odds against the Delian League's impressive array of armed might. Yet by its very nature such a confrontation between groups of allies posed a serious threat to all parties. In the past, wars fought among the Greeks rarely involved more than two or three poleis at a time and usually resulted in minimal long-term damage. But now entire leagues of cities were facing off, and the whole Greek world was polarizing, or becoming divided into two. Victor Ehrenberg describes the breakdown:

[Athenian] imperialism and democracy worked hand in hand against Sparta's old . . . oligarchy; the Greeks were forced into the position of taking sides, neutrality was no longer really possible, and among the ruling oligarchies of some of the [pro-Spartan] allied states the fear of Athenian rule must have grown. The great division, the dualism of the Greek world, became inevitable, and if a man like Cimon had believed in an ideal of balance between the two great powers . . . that had lost its meaning for a long time.[39]

The Athenians Provoke Their Enemies

Luckily for all involved, the inevitable all-out war between the leagues was still a generation away. For the moment, Athenian aggression provoked a series of periodic, isolated battles, sieges, and short military campaigns that historians sometimes refer to collectively as the First Peloponnesian War. Sparta itself played only a small direct role, and most of the fighting was between Athens and a handful of Spartan allies.

The trouble began when Athens allied itself to Argos and Thessaly in 461 B.C., shortly before Ephialtes was assassinated. Argos and Thessaly hated Sparta, which had bullied them both in the 470s, so the alliances were clearly an insult hurled at the Spartans by the leaders of Athens's new democratic regime. Another such insult was not long in coming. This time Athens boldly involved itself in an ongoing dispute between two important members of the Peloponnesian League. One was Corinth, already resentful of Athenian infringements on its commerce, and the other was Megara, which bordered Corinth on the northern end of the strategic isthmus. The Athenians seized the town of Naupactus, on the northern shore of the Gulf of Corinth. This, says Bury, "secured a naval station which gave Athens a considerable control over the mouth of the [gulf]. . . . Athens now had the means of intercepting and harassing the Corinthian argosies [merchant ships] which sailed forth with merchandise for the far west."[40]

As Corinth went to war against Athens, the latter struck still another blow at the pride of Sparta and the Peloponnesian League. Because of their dispute with the Corinthians, in 459 the Megarians decided to quit the Peloponnesian League and the Athenians promptly invited them to join the rival Delian League. Wasting no time, Athens began building a large defensive wall across the isthmus in Megarian territory. Since the barrier would make it impossible for any of the Peloponnesians to travel northward into Attica or the rest of Greece, Sparta viewed this move as a blatant act of war.

For the time being, however, the Spartans held back and let their Corinthian allies do the fighting. After a few relatively indecisive skirmishes, Corinth acquired a welcome ally, the little island of Aegina, located in the middle of the Saronic Gulf directly south of Attica. Aegina's small size belied its importance. Its coinage, the first to appear in mainland Greece, had once been the standard for Aegean trade, and the island remained one of the wealthiest and busiest centers of maritime commerce in Greece. Not surprisingly, relations between Athens and Aegina, longtime rivals, grew increasingly bitter. Pericles himself called Aegina "the eyesore of the Piraeus"[41] referring to the fact that the island is plainly visible from Athens's port, and called for his countrymen to remove that eyesore.

The Defeat of Aegina

For their part, the Aeginetans were just as eager to remove the threat of Piraeus's large naval yards, especially with Corinth under Athenian attack. Fearing that if Corinth lost, Aegina would be Athens's next target, the Aeginetans joined Corinth in the struggle. In 458, Athens, aided by several of its allies, fought and defeated Aegina in a large sea battle in the Saronic Gulf. After capturing over seventy enemy ships, the Athenians, commanded by Leocrates, landed on Aegina and began a

Tiny but Powerful Aegina

The fighting in the early 450s B.C. between Athens and Aegina, close neighbors who had been longtime rivals in Aegean commerce, was hard and bitter. In this excerpt from his scholarly work, The Rise of the Greeks, *classical historian Michael Grant gives a thumbnail sketch of ancient Aegina.*

"This mountainous, volcanic and somewhat unapproachable island lay in the Saronic Gulf, midway between Attica and the Peloponnesus, occupying a position which, despite its small size of only thirty-two square miles, had guaranteed its importance in Mediterranean commerce from the earliest periods. . . . Aegina avoided the phase of dictatorial government that occurred at other cities, and developed a stable oligarchic, mercantile regime. Under this administration, the Aeginetans not only developed a profitable . . . pedlar trade, but became, in the seventh century [B.C.], a Greek sea power of the first order. From ca. 595/590, or perhaps a little later, they began to issue silver coins with the design of a turtle, the earliest of all coinages in or near the mainland. [This money] circulated widely for centuries to come, establishing one of the two principal monetary weight-standards [along with the Athenian drachma] of the Greeks. . . . Aegina also developed the oldest system of weights and measures known in the Greek world. . . . It was Athens which inevitably schemed to break the naval and commercial success of the uncomfortably close Aeginetans. . . . Between the oligarchy which controlled Aegina and the more democratically inclined Athenians there was no common ground."

siege of its fortified main city. Eventually, the Aeginetans had no choice but to surrender, after which Athens forced them to join the Delian League and to pay huge sums of yearly tribute. Meanwhile, another Athenian *strategos*, Myronides, intercepted and crushed a force of Corinthian hoplites that had been attempting to invade Megara. Corinth, like Aegina, languished in defeat.

For the Athenians, nearly two years of fighting on fronts stretching from Greece to Egypt had been mostly successful. The enormous scope of both their enterprises and their sacrifices is evident from a gravestone left behind by one of Athens's ten tribes. The inscription reads: "Of the Erechtheid tribe, these are they who died in the war in Cyprus, in Egypt, in Phoenicia [the Palestinian coasts east of Cyprus], in Aegina, at Megara, in the same year."[42] Following these words are 177 Athenian names.

The Battle of Tanagra

Athens's string of military successes alarmed and enraged the Spartans. But nothing angered them more than another Athenian affront, this one engineered by Pericles while Athens was besieging Aegina. The Athenian *strategoi* realized that sooner or later the dreaded Spartan phalanx would make a move on their city, which lacked adequate defenses. The walls Themistocles had built might protect Athens for a while, but an invading army could simply camp outside the walls and starve the city into submission. Land-locked Athens needed a way to tap into its naval lifeline at Piraeus. So in the summer of 458 B.C. Pericles began work on what immediately became known as the "Long Walls," a defensive perimeter that stretched the whole five miles to the port of Piraeus. These walls formed a safe-access corridor to the sea and permitted a virtually unlimited flow of food and other

The port of Piraeus, and Athens. The Acropolis complex is visible in the distance at the end of the Long Walls.

A modern sketch depicts the ruins on the site of ancient Thebes, once one of Greece's most powerful city-states and a frequent arch-rival of Athens.

supplies. "The completion of this construction," comments Donald Kagan, turned "Athens into an island unassailable by land and invincible so long as it retained command of the sea."[43]

Pericles and his colleagues had been right. The Spartans were eager to punish and contain the "arrogant" Athenians and considered sending an army into Attica. But the walls the Athenians had erected on the Megarian frontier and the Long Walls encasing Athens and Piraeus formed a double barrier that even the Spartans dared not attempt to penetrate. The solution to the dilemma, the Spartans reasoned, was to attack Athens from its only exposed flank—Attica's northern border. This was Boeotian territory, dominated by the Thebans, who still hated Athens for

defeating them at the close of the preceding century.

It was with visions of revenge on Athens, then, that in the summer of 457 Thebes welcomed the arrival of a force of fifteen hundred Spartan hoplites and some ten thousand Peloponnesian allies. The army had entered Boeotia from the west after crossing the Gulf of Corinth. No doubt the plan was for Thebes and its allies to join the Peloponnesians in an invasion of Attica. But the Athenians foiled the plan by quickly and boldly marching their own army to the Boeotian frontier. Counting perhaps fifteen hundred allies from Thessaly and from the Argolid, the Athenian force totaled about fourteen thousand hoplites. The opposing phalanxes faced each other on a hot summer

A Terrible Cacophony

The battles of Tanagra and Oenophyta, like other clashes between opposing Greek phalanxes, were marked not only by gory displays of blood, severed limbs, and bodies, but also by a deafening mix of unusual and frightening noises. Noted classical historian Victor David Hanson describes the sounds of war in this tract from his book, The Western Way of War: Infantry Battle in Classical Greece.

"The entire noise of men and equipment was concentrated onto the small area of the ancient battlefield—itself usually a small plain encircled by mountains, which only improved the acoustics [sound transmission]. . . . It was not just that the decibel level [loudness] of Greek battle increased as the two phalanxes neared and met. The *nature* of the sound also changed from that of recognizable human speech—the war cry or song . . . to a terrible cacophony [din] of smashed bronze, wood, and flesh. Very early on in Greek literature we learn that the ancients were well aware of this particular inhuman sound of death. In the *Iliad*, for example, there are over half a dozen . . . words for fighting or battle that can only be translated as 'roar' or 'thud,' the sounds which arose after the two sides finally crashed together. . . . The Greeks recognized that the peculiar noise of this initial crash came from a variety of sources. First, there was the dull thud of bronze against wood as either the metal spear point made its way through the wood core of a hoplite shield, or as soldiers struck their shields against the bronze breastplates and helmets of the enemy, or as wooden shield was bashed into shield. . . . The live sounds were more animal-like than human: the concerted groans of men exerting themselves, pushing forward in group effort with their bodies and shields against the immovable armor of the enemy. . . . Finally, there were all too often the noises of human misery. Here arose a tortured symphony of shrieks as a man went down with a wound to the groin, the steady sobbing of a soldier in extremis [dying], a final gasp of fright as the spear thrust found its way home."

afternoon near Tanagra, about twenty miles east of Thebes.

Shortly before the onset of battle, a surprise visitor arrived in the Athenian camp. It was Cimon, arrayed in full armor and eager to demonstrate his patriotism. According to Plutarch, he

placed himself in the line of battle by the side of the men of his tribe, determined to clear himself of his supposed pro-Spartan sympathies by his actions and by sharing the dangers of his fellow countrymen. However, Pericles' friends combined to drive Cimon away from the ranks on the ground that he was still an exile.[44]

Cimon reluctantly departed, but not before admonishing his friends, who were also suspected of being pro-Spartan, to fight bravely to prove their own patriotism. Soon afterward, in a mighty crash of shields and spears and a din of raised voices, the battle was joined. Cimon's friends, Plutarch recorded,

grouped themselves into a single company, fought with desperate courage and were finally killed to the last man, 100 of them all told. The Athenians bitterly lamented their loss and were plunged into remorse for having so unjustly accused them. For this reason the people's resentment against Cimon quickly died down.[45]

The Spartans and their allies won a slim victory that day at Tanagra. But they did not follow up on their success. Perhaps realizing that tough Athenian resistance would make an invasion of Attica a very long affair, the Spartans returned to the

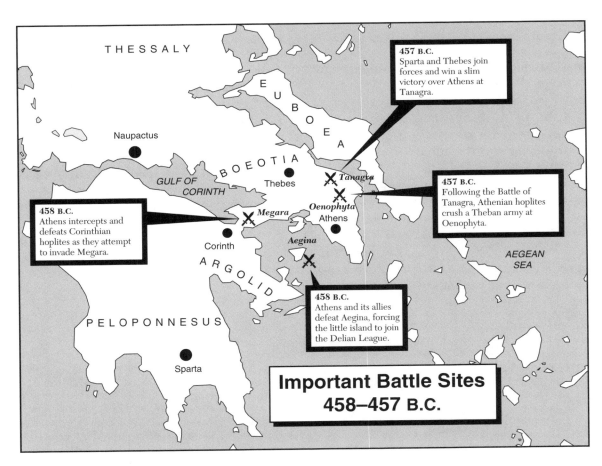

457 B.C. Sparta and Thebes join forces and win a slim victory over Athens at Tanagra.

457 B.C. Following the Battle of Tanagra, Athenian hoplites crush a Theban army at Oenophyta.

458 B.C. Athens intercepts and defeats Corinthian hoplites as they attempt to invade Megara.

458 B.C. Athens and its allies defeat Aegina, forcing the little island to join the Delian League.

Important Battle Sites 458–457 B.C.

Peloponnesus. They went by the land route across the isthmus, taking the opportunity to ravage Megarian villages and farms along the way. Their sudden and unexpected departure left a power vacuum along the Boeotian frontier, which the opportunistic Athenians hastened to fill. Just two months after the battle at Tanagra, Myronides led a force of hoplites to Oenophyta, a few miles south of Tanagra, and decisively defeated an army made up of Thebans and their allies. Once more Athens had punished Thebes, gaining control over most of Boeotia in the process.

A Serious Reversal of Fortunes

In the first half of the 450s B.C. Athens had managed to expand or at least to maintain its power status both on land and at sea. But the second half of the decade witnessed a serious reversal of its fortunes, mainly because the Egyptian expedition collapsed unexpectedly. In 456 Artaxerxes launched a massive counteroffensive against the rebels, drove the Greeks from Memphis, and besieged them on a Nile island. There, in 454, the Persians wiped out the entire Greek force, over two hundred ships and at least forty thousand men. As Meiggs explains:

> This was a disaster of the greatest magnitude for Athens. . . . Its psychological impact must have been even more damaging than the loss of men and ships. It broke an uninterrupted series of Athenian victories over Persia, caused serious unrest in the Aegean, and forced a curtailment of the Athenian efforts on the [Greek] mainland.[46]

In the wake of the catastrophe, Athenian leaders realized, the eastern Mediterranean and Aegean waters were, at least for the time being, vulnerable to Persian attack. Worried about the safety of the Delian League's treasury on Delos, Pericles ordered the monies transferred directly to Athens. This immediately caused an uproar, not only among the other league members, but among many Athenians as well. They charged that Pericles was a thief, who planned to use the money as he and his colleagues saw fit without regard for Athens's allies. Pericles' political opponents, Plutarch wrote,

> cried out in the Assembly that Athens had lost her good name and disgraced herself by transferring from Delos . . . the funds that had been contributed by the rest of Greece. . . . "The Greeks must be outraged," they cried. "They must consider this an act of bare-faced tyranny.". . . Pericles' answer to the people was that the Athenians were not obliged to give the allies any account of how their money was spent. . . . "They do not give us a single horse, nor a soldier, nor a ship. All they supply is money," he told the Athenians, "and this belongs not to the people who give it, but to those who receive it, so long as they provide the services they are paid for."[47]

Pericles was really saying that Athens was strong enough to take and use the money, and there was nothing the other league members could do about it. Some historians mark this moment as the official beginning of the Athenian empire.

Meanwhile, temporarily weakened by the Egyptian disaster, Athens could not afford to risk any new and costly battles with

Soldiers like these members of the Persian king's royal guard, depicted on a relief set on a brick wall from a Persian palace, helped to defeat the Athenian Egyptian expedition.

Sparta. Seeking peace, in 451 the Athenians called upon Cimon, now back from exile, to arrange a truce, "for the Spartans," wrote Plutarch, "were as well disposed towards him as they were hostile to Pericles and the other democratic leaders."[48] Cimon convinced the Spartans to agree to a five-year truce. And so, Athens acquired a breathing space in which to recover from its losses, consolidate its gain, and concentrate on beautifying the city. History would remember the latter most of all.

4 Democracy and Imperialism: A City Thrown Open to the World

Athenian leaders were well aware that the five-year truce with Sparta, arranged in 451 B.C. by Cimon, was a shaky one. Sparta and its allies might break it at any time and launch a devastating land war. At the same time, after regaining Egypt, the Persians boldly resumed their assault on the island of Cyprus. Because the island could

In this depiction of a legendary event, a group of Greek soldiers who have been fighting in western Persia discover the tomb of the ancient Athenian hero Theseus.

be used as a base from which to launch attacks on the Greek islands, Persia once again posed a threat to the Aegean, the center of Athenian power and commerce. Underscoring this threat, in 450, only a year after his return from exile, Cimon died while leading an anti-Persian military expedition in Cyprus. His loss made it clearer than ever that the only realistic way for Athens to maintain the security of its empire and democracy was to seek permanent peace with both Persia and Sparta.

Athens attained the first half of this goal in 449. The Peace of Callias, so named because Cimon's brother-in-law Callias negotiated it, at long last ended more than a half-century of hostilities between the Greeks and Persians. According to the first-century B.C. Greek historian Diodorus, the treaty contained the following stipulations:

> All the Greek cities of Asia [Minor] are to be independent [of Persian rule]; no Persian province is to come closer than a three-days' journey from the [Mediterranean] sea. . . . If the [Persian] King and his generals respect these terms, the Athenians are not to send any expedition against the country over which the King rules.[49]

Basically, the treaty affirmed that the Aegean sphere was solely a Greek dominion.

Three years later, in 446, Athens concluded a similar treaty with Sparta. In the so-called Thirty Years Peace, the Athenians agreed to stay out of Peloponnesian affairs and in return the Spartans formally recognized the political reality of Athens's empire. Both parties recognized that Greece was permanently divided into two blocs and agreed that no member of one alliance should be allowed to change sides. It is important to note that the successful maintenance of this peace did not rest on goodwill or the concept of mending fences. Athens and Sparta clearly recognized that they would remain enemies with irreconcilable differences. The peace would last only if the parties maintained a "balance of power" in which each one refrained from expanding into the other's territory. The question on everyone's mind was: Could the ever restless Athenians learn to restrain themselves and to tend to their own affairs?

Pericles and His Rivals

At first, thanks to the peace afforded by the treaties, Athens did seem to channel much of its abundant energy into domestic affairs and problems. At the top of the political agenda was the ongoing development of democracy, which had been expanding in stages since Solon's time. Pericles and his partisans vigorously promoted further democratic reforms, while a hard core of conservatives and aristocrats just as vigorously argued that oligarchy should be reinstated. Pericles and his supporters had managed to push through some solid reforms in their first decade in power. Now, in the new era of peace, they tried hard to build on these reforms, to continue to make Athens's democratic institutions ever more liberal and open.

What motivated the democrats' great zeal for reform? Plutarch's attempt to answer this question in his *Life of Pericles* is revealing. In the following biographical

A Passion for Statesmanship

In this excerpt from his penetrating study of classical Greece, From Solon to Socrates, *historian Victor Ehrenberg offers this character sketch of Pericles.*

"What sort of man Pericles really was is very hard to discover. Neither Thucydides' nor Plutarch's portrait can be called unbiased and authentic; in particular, neither of them distinguished between the earlier and the later Pericles. It was only the latter they knew, and that is more or less true of our knowledge too. . . . The Pericles of the 'fifties and the early 'forties [B.C.]. . . . grew steadily more cautious as well as more autocratic. The 'Olympian' [one of his nicknames], no doubt, was a lonely man. Among the politicians, including his supporters, he had no friend. He avoided all social activity, he did not leave any written records, he only went out [of his home] for official business, and his speeches were always impressive. . . . He did not speak of the gods, nor indeed of any traditional beliefs. He showed reverence when and where it was needed, but had no piety in the sense that people understood it, and it was this aspect that played a decisive part in the attitude of his opponents [who called him an atheist]. . . . The only passion in Pericles' austere and reserved mind was statesmanship, which included day-to-day politics. The people in general trusted him, not least because of his integrity in financial matters, a quality comparably rare among Greek politicians."

excerpt, Pericles appears to embrace democracy partly in a sincere attempt to help the underprivileged but also as a means of enhancing his own prestige and power:

As a young man Pericles was inclined to shrink from facing the people. . . . The fact that he was rich and that he came of a distinguished family and possessed exceedingly powerful

friends made the fear of ostracism very real to him, and at the beginning of his career he took no part in politics but devoted himself to soldiering, in which he showed a great daring and enterprise. However, the time came when . . . Themistocles [was] in exile, and Cimon frequently absent on distant campaigns. Then at last Pericles decided to attach himself to the people's party and to take up the cause of the poor and the many instead of that of the rich and the few, in spite of the fact that this was quite contrary to his own temperament, which was thoroughly aristocratic. He was afraid, apparently, of being suspected of aiming at a dictatorship; so when he saw that Cimon's sympathies were strongly with the nobles and that he was the idol of the aristocratic party, he [Pericles] began to ingratiate himself [become friendly and close] with the people, partly for self-preservation and partly by way of securing power against his rival.[50]

Initially, Pericles' main rival, of course, was Cimon, who was as conservative and pro-Spartan as the democrats were liberal and anti-Spartan. Even while in exile in the 450s B.C., Cimon remained a potent force in Athenian politics, for his influential relatives and friends carried on the opposition to the democrats. But when he died fighting in Cyprus in 450, the conservatives needed a strong figure to replace him. They chose Thucydides (not the historian), a politician who disapproved of open democracy and distrusted this form of government. According to Plutarch:

> The aristocratic party had already recognized for some time that Pericles was now the most important man in Athens and . . . they were anxious that there should be someone . . . capable of standing up to him so as to blunt the edge of his authority and prevent it from becoming an outright monarchy. They therefore put forward Thucydides, of Alopece, a man of good sense and a relative of Cimon [perhaps his brother-in-law], to lead the opposition. . . . He soon succeeded

in creating a balance of power in Athenian affairs.[51]

Some scholars suspect that Thucydides might have been the "Old Oligarch," the name traditionally given to the anonymous author of a surviving Athenian document known as *The Constitution of the Athenians*. This manuscript attacks liberal democracy as unstable and dangerous because it is driven by the whims of the "ignorant and untrustworthy masses." Regardless of whether Thucydides was actually the author, the document almost certainly reflects the views he and his supporters advocated. The Old Oligarch states that he does not approve of the democrats' system because

> they have given the advantages to the vulgar people at the cost of the

Pericles as he may have looked when in his forties or fifties.

A speaker (center) attempts to win the attention of patrons in this bustling public square. Without other forms of media, speakers were forced to rely upon oratory to persuade citizens and obtain votes.

good. . . . They everywhere give the vulgar and the poor and the common people the preference to the aristocrats. . . . In every country [in which] the aristocracy is contrasted to the democracy, there [can be seen] in the best people [aristocrats] the least immorality and wickedness, but the keenest eyes for morals; in the people on the other hand we find a very high degree of ignorance, disorder, and vileness; for poverty more and more leads them in the direction of bad morals.[52]

Swayed by Oratory

The dramatic rivalry between democrats like Pericles and conservatives like Thucy-

dides was most evident in meetings of the Assembly. On the Pnyx hill, in sight of the Athenian Acropolis, about every ten days thousands of citizens gathered to hear and act on speeches delivered by prominent politicians. Leaders on both sides knew that the stakes in such political oratory were high. In an age without newspapers and electronic media, Greek politicians had to sway the voters directly. Speeches had to be very persuasive, and the policies advocated had to bring prompt, measurable results, or voters were likely to turn to the views and policies of a speaker's opponents. As Michael Grant explains:

The loud say . . . possessed by every citizen sometimes meant that a burst of eloquence [fine oratory] could carry away a whole gathering into united, impulsive action. . . . The flashpoint

"Fix Your Eyes upon the Greatness of Athens"

Brilliant and moving oratory was one of the methods Pericles used to win the support of a majority of Athenians year after year. The power of these speeches to inspire patriotism is apparent in this excerpt (quoted in Athens in the Age of Pericles *by Charles Robinson) from his well-known funeral oration over a group of Athenian war dead. After a lengthy description of the city's many glorious qualities and achievements, Pericles continued:*

"I have dwelt upon the greatness of Athens because I want to show you that we are contending for a higher prize than those who enioy none of these privileges, and to establish by much proof the merit of these men I am now commemorating. Their loftiest praise has already been spoken. For in magnifying the city I have magnified them, and men like them whose virtues made her glorious. . . . I would have you day by day fix your eyes upon the greatness of Athens, until you become filled with the love of her; and when you are impressed by the spectacle of her glory, reflect that this empire has been acquired by men who knew their duty and had the courage to do it, who in the hour of conflict had the fear of dishonor always present to them, and who, if ever they failed in an enterprise, would not allow their virtues to be lost to their country, but freely gave their lives to her as the fairest offering which they could present at her feast."

Pericles addresses his countrymen in his famous funeral oration, a speech in which he extolled Athens's virtues.

was low, and either one's own or one's opponent's view was quickly acted upon, with . . . immediate repercussions [consequences].[53]

Both the democrats and the conservatives gave persuasive reasons for the voters to support their respective policies. As one might expect, Pericles took every opportunity to sing the praises of open political institutions that gave all people, even the poor, a say in deciding their destiny. The rewards of democracy were obvious, he said, and the citizens could easily see how great Athens had become under that system:

> Because of the greatness of our city, the fruits of the whole earth flow in upon us so that we enjoy the goods of other countries as freely as our own. . . . Our city is thrown open to the world, and we never expel a foreigner. . . . And in the matter of education . . . we live at ease and yet are equally ready to face perils to which our strength is equal. . . . Nor is this the only cause for marveling at our city. We are lovers of beauty without extravagance and of learning. . . . Wealth we employ less for talk . . . than when there is a real use for it. To avow poverty with us is no disgrace: the true disgrace is doing nothing to avoid it. The same persons attend at once to the concerns of their households and of the city, and men of diverse employments have a very fair idea of politics. If a man takes no interest in public affairs, we . . . do not commend him as quiet but condemn him as useless. . . . To sum up, I say that the whole city is an education for Greece. . . . This is no passing boast in speech, but . . . veri-

fied by the actual power of the city which we have won by this way of life.[54]

Greece's Tyrant?

But was liberal democracy truly the "way of life" that had made Athens great? Thucydides and his colleagues argued that the city's wealth, its inflow of goods, and the leisure time that allowed so many citizens to take part in government were more the result of Athenian imperialism. Athens enjoyed "the goods of other countries," they said, because it employed military force to control and regulate the commerce of the subject states in its empire. This made the city not the "education for Greece," but rather, Greece's tyrant. Painting Pericles as a tyrant, in fact, was the conservatives' chief tactic in their attempt to discredit the democratic faction and its leader. According to Donald Kagan:

> What Thucydides would have liked to proclaim was a program to roll back the democratic revolution of Ephialtes. . . . [In order to] make what was a democracy in name into an aristocracy in fact . . . issues must be found which were acceptable to a democratic people, which would discredit Pericles, and which would attract support to the party of Thucydides. . . . To destroy a politician in a democracy it is well to discredit him personally. . . . In Athens the most damaging charge that could be made against a democratic politician was that he aimed at tyranny. . . . [According to Thucydides, Pericles] avoided public occasions . . . associated

with suspicious intellectuals, held uncommon religious views, and consorted regularly with foreign men and women. . . . It was easy enough to persuade some people that such a man was on the way to establishing a tyranny.[55]

In particular, the conservatives denounced Pericles' "theft" of the Delian League's treasury and his open use of the funds to improve and beautify Athens. But on this issue the public criticism leveled against Pericles had little negative effect overall on him or his party. While many Athenians admitted that his use of the funds was not exactly ethical, most were not willing to give up the obvious benefits

of such diversions. Thus, Pericles' continuous strategy of extolling Athens's greatness and the comfortable life within its borders paid off. As long as the city was the most open, prosperous, and beautiful in Greece, he maintained the popular support he needed to carry on the democratic revolution begun by Ephialtes, much to the disappointment of Thucydides and the conservatives.

Full Citizen Participation

The initial achievement of that revolution had been the demotion of the aristocratic

In this modern drawing, an architect, possibly Ictinus, shows a construction plan to Pericles, who periodically oversaw various stages of the city's beautification.

The Secret of Pericles' Power

In this tract from his Life of Pericles *(translated in* The Rise and Fall of Athens: Nine Greek Lives*), Plutarch comments on how Pericles became an autocratic but incorruptible father figure after the ostracism of his chief opponent, Thucydides of Alopece.*

"From this point political opposition was at an end, the parties had merged themselves into one, and the city presented a single and unbroken front. Pericles now proceeded to bring under his own control not only home affairs, but all issues in which the authority of Athens was involved; these included matters of tribute, the army, the navy, the islands, maritime affairs, the great resources which Athens derived both from the Greek states and from the barbarians [non-Greeks]. . . . But at the same time Pericles' own conduct took on quite a different character. . . . He abandoned the somewhat . . . indulgent [lenient] leadership he had shown on occasion . . . and struck instead the firm, high note of an aristocratic, even regal [kingly] statesmanship. And since he used his authority honestly and unswervingly in the interests of the city, he was usually able to carry the people with him by rational argument and persuasion. . . . There were, as might be expected, all kinds of disorders to be found among a mass of citizens who possessed an empire as great as that of Athens, and Pericles was the only man capable of keeping each of these under control. . . . The secret of Pericles' power depended . . . not merely upon his oratory, but upon the reputation . . . he enjoyed as a man who had proved himself completely indifferent to bribes. Great as Athens had been when he became her leader, he made her the greatest and richest of all cities, and he came to hold more power in his hands than many a king and tyrant."

Areopagus in 461 B.C. This had left the Assembly and the Council as the most powerful and influential state institutions. In that same year, the democrats, guided by Pericles, began addressing the problem of citizen participation in government. Though Athens's legislature was democra-

tic, a large portion of the citizenry, mainly those with moderate to low incomes, were excluded from serving the state. Most were barred by law from holding high office. And even more modest or temporary service, such as jury duty, was out of reach because government positions were unpaid. The poor simply could not afford to leave their jobs long enough to serve. So Pericles proposed and passed a bill that provided payment for jurors. Charles Robinson comments:

> Juries are probably the cornerstone of any democracy, and at Athens no less than six thousand jurors were selected every year. By giving them a daily wage, Pericles completely democratized the juries, since now even the poorest members could serve regularly. Indeed, the typical juror was an old man, and Pericles' proposal was in effect a form of old-age pension.[56]

The next reforms occurred in the 450s. One was the elimination of one of Solon's old laws, which stipulated that only people who met certain financial qualifications could hold high office. The democrats thereby opened the high administrative post of archon to anyone who desired it. Soon afterward, the method of choosing candidates for the archonship and for the Council also underwent reform. Such candidates were now chosen completely by lot, or random drawing. J. B. Bury explains:

> [The use of] lot had been long ago introduced; but it had not been introduced in its purest form. The archons and other lesser officers, and the members of the Council, were taken by lot from a select number of candidates; but these candidates [all wealthy or aristocratic] were chosen by deliberate election. This mixed system was now abolished; the preliminary election was now done away with; and the Council of Five Hundred, as well as the archons, were appointed by lot

from all the eligible citizens. By this means every citizen had an equal chance of holding political office, and taking a part in the conduct of public affairs.[57]

One side effect of ceasing to elect the archons was a reduction in their authority, since the people tended to entrust more power to officials they personally selected. Thereafter, the ten *strategoi*, who continued to be selected by direct popular election, were by far the most powerful and influential state leaders. No doubt the conservatives accused Pericles and the other generals of manipulating the system to increase their own power. But even if this charge had any foundation, it was outweighed by the several real and substantial reforms that had benefited all the people. "The central fact about Periclean Athens," writes Robinson, "was the full participation of its citizens in the government of city and empire."[58]

An Appetite for Expansion

Indeed, personal motives aside, available evidence suggests that Pericles and his supporters sincerely believed that democracy was good for Athens and its people. Like all democrats then and later, they also insisted that the system would be good for everyone else as well. And so, they encouraged and helped build democracies in other poleis. But in this case the Pericleans' motives were not so unselfish. By exporting democracy, the Athenians sought to strengthen their influence over other Greek states, the theory being that smaller democracies would look to Athens as their parent and guide. Sparta kept a watchful eye on these activities to make sure that Athens did not try to convert any of the states in the Peloponnesian alliance. Interfering in the Spartan sphere would constitute a clear violation of the Thirty Years Peace.

But if Athens did not violate the treaty in fact, it certainly did so in spirit. In the decade of the 440s B.C. it found a means by which it could feed its appetite for expansion without resorting to obvious military means. The key was the establishment of cleruchies. "A cleruchy, unlike a colony," explains Kagan, "was a settlement of Athenians on land taken from another people. The settlers did not make up a new independent city [as colonists did] but remained Athenian citizens, often living side by side with the natives."[59] In 450 Athens set up a cleruchy on Naxos, which it had subjugated nearly two decades before. Two other Aegean islands, Andros and Lemnos, also received Athenian cleruchies that same year. Soon afterward a similar settlement sprang up in the Thracian Chersonese, and in 443 another appeared at Thurii in southern Italy.

The impact of the cleruchies was twofold. Between 450 and 440, over 4,000 Athenians received tracts of land abroad and many thousands of merchants, artisans, and laborers emigrated with them. Clearly, setting up cleruchies helped to relieve the pressures due to Athens's rapidly growing population. By 450 Attica had at least 265,000 inhabitants, more than ten times as many as the average Greek polis. But more ominously, the cleruchies also constituted new outposts in the city's still-expanding empire. Recognizing the potential of these settlements as Athenian military bases, the Spartans viewed the cleruchy program with increasing apprehension.

In 443 Sparta found still more to worry about, in this case the sudden demise of the Athenian conservatives. For a long time, Thucydides and his supporters had tried to slow the trend toward complete democracy, which both they and the Spartans viewed as radical and dangerous. Eventually, however, the conservatives' attacks on Pericles backfired. The people saw clearly that his use of the Delian League's funds was a boon to the city and they grew tired of hearing Thucydides condemn this policy. Finally, recorded Plutarch,

> Pericles ventured to put matters to a test of an ostracism, and the result was that he secured his rival's banishment and the disintegration of the [conservative] party. . . . From this point political opposition was at an end, the parties had merged themselves into one, and the city presented a single and unbroken front.[60]

That front was staunchly democratic and imperialistic. And at its head stood Pericles, now the most powerful single person in the Greek world, yearning to lead Athens into new and glorious adventures.

5 The Classic Achievement: Athens Reaches Its Cultural Zenith

After the signing of the Thirty Years Peace with Sparta, Attica's frontiers with the members of the Peloponnesian League remained relatively quiet in the 440s and early 430s B.C. The lull afforded by the truce allowed Athens to concentrate on domestic political issues, particularly the maintenance of democracy. During the same years the Athenians also expended a great deal of energy and money enlarging and beautifying Athens, Piraeus, and other parts of Attica. The crowning achievement of this effort was a massive building program that produced some of the most magnificent structures ever erected. These included new temples, statues, and a monumental entrance gate atop Athens's Acropolis. At the time, the Acropolis complex, including the famous Parthenon, dedicated to the goddess Athena, was more than a great architectural and artistic achievement. It stood as a symbol of Athenian imperial power, a reminder to other poleis, and to non-Greeks as well, that Athens was favored and blessed by the gods, an invincible and eternal city.

As it has with all other cities and nations, history showed that Athens was not invincible. But in a very real way the

In this vista of ancient Athens can be seen many of the ambitious building projects Pericles instituted, including the splendid Parthenon atop the Acropolis.

Acropolis complex did turn out to be eternal. Long after Greek power in the Mediterranean world had faded, these structures survived as a tribute not only to the great Athenian artists of the Periclean age, but as a symbol of all the noble qualities of the ancient Greeks as a people. For in the mid-fifth century B.C. Athens became the focus of a sudden, amazing, and ultimately immortal outburst of Greek art, literature, and culture.

"In the space of less than three generations of this fifth century," comments Michael Grant, the Athenians "excelled at tragic drama, history, philosophy, sculpture, architecture and painting. This simultaneous classic achievement in so huge a variety of fields was startling and unequalled." This marvelous accomplishment would not have been possible, of course, without the expenditure of vast sums of money. It was the way that Athens got the money—collecting it from its subject states "at swordpoint" so to speak—that detracted from the nobility of the accomplishment. Grant continues:

A Blend of Old and New

The first edifice a visitor to the ancient Athenian Acropolis encountered was the magnificent entranceway, the Propylaea. It was designed by the architect Mnesicles and built between 437 and 432 B.C. This brief description is from The Classical Greeks, *by Michael Grant.*

"The building consisted of a large square three-aisled hall, pierced by five gateways reached by five steps, with the exception of the central gateway, which was approached by an inclined ramp. The Propylaea blends the traditional, solid Doric Order of architecture with the more slender delicate Ionic. The new amalgam [blend] was not without contemporary significance, since whereas the Doric was still reminiscent of the Peloponnesus, of which Sparta was the leader, the Ionic—which had hardly ever been seen before to the west of the Aegean—recalled Athens's claim to be the founder and leader of all the Greek cities of Ionia in western Asia Minor. The blend of the two orders was introduced by retaining Doric for the six-column porticoes [porches] that face inwards and outwards, whereas the columns dividing the hall were Ionic, and the outer porch of the avenue spanned by the central gateway was flanked by colonnades of the same order. Mnesicles also added wings projecting from the front, faced with Doric columns. The north wing contained a square chamber which served as a picture-gallery, its walls painted by Polygnotus and other artists."

Depicted here is a part of the Propylaea, the magnificent entranceway leading onto the heights of the Acropolis, on which stood the imposing structures that became instant symbols both of Athenian power and prestige and of the Greek creative spirit in general.

The Athenians felt impelled to imperial enterprises because such a wonderful civilization . . . could not be maintained without wealth. And they were inspired by the added belief . . . that this was all being done for all Greece: because, as Pericles reminded them, Athens was an education for the entire country.[61]

And so, even as they produced the culture that showed off a remarkable civilization, the Athenians revealed a darker side by continuing to rule their empire with an iron hand. The tensions and hatreds they generated in doing so would have tragic consequences later.

Greece's Power and Glory

Beginning in the mid-440s B.C., much of the money from the Delian League treasury went into Athens's ambitious new building program. According to Plutarch's account of this era:

There was one measure above all which at once gave the greatest pleasure to the Athenians, adorned their city and created amazement among the rest of mankind, and which is today [the first century A.D., in which Plutarch lived] the sole testimony that the tales of the ancient power and glory of Greece are no mere fables. By this I mean his [Pericles'] construction of temples and public buildings.[62]

Since the Acropolis was the visual and ceremonial heart of the polis, it became the scene of the most lavish improvements. The original Parthenon and other temples on the citadel had been destroyed by the Persians when they had briefly occupied the city in 480. In their place now rose structures on a much grander scale. Laboring day after day, year after year, an army of architects, stonemasons, carpenters, and sculptors transformed the irregular gray, rocky summit into a spectacular vision of form and color. The materials used, Plutarch reported, "were stone, bronze, ivory, gold, ebony, and cypress-wood." The artisans who modeled these substances, he

wrote, were supported by thousands of merchants, sailors, animal drivers, wagon makers, and road builders. "Each individual craft, like a general with an army under his separate command, had its own corps of unskilled laborers at its disposal."[63]

The fruits of this labor, the completed Acropolis complex, was, John Crow writes, "the heart and soul of what has survived of the Golden Age of Greek art." According to Crow, even today, in a state of ruin, the complex remains an awesome creation: "The spectator is never disappointed, the imagination is never deceived, the anticipation is never dismayed. Every [person] deserves to look at least once upon this sight before he dies."[64] In its original form, of course, the complex was even more splendid. It was fronted by a huge and magnificent entranceway—the Propy-

The Parthenon, pictured here shortly after its completion, was perhaps the most famous and structurally perfect building ever constructed.

laea. Close by this column-lined portal, on the citadel's summit, stood three temples—the Erechthium, the Temple of Wingless Victory, and the new Parthenon.

A New Vision of Life

Begun in the 440s B.C. and completed in 438 B.C., the Parthenon instantly became the wonder of the world. Designed by the architect Ictinus and the master sculptor Phidias, it was 237 feet long, 110 feet wide, and over 60 feet high. More than twenty-two thousand tons of exquisite marble went into its construction. Inside stood a huge statue of the goddess Athena and outside were several stone altars at which citizens worshiped her. At once simple and ornate, possessing both serene reserve and bold audacity, the Parthenon was a visual expression of Athens's unique spirit. What makes the building so special, suggests Greek scholar John Miliadis in his book *The Acropolis*,

> is the feeling of life that springs up from the immortal work. . . . The Parthenon . . . is clear reasoning, and yet filled with humanity; it is not directed to the mind so much as to the eye and the soul; it means to move the spirit and to ennoble it. It is more like a living organism than a mechanical creation. It is more the work of inspiration than of calculation. It is a new vision of life, the vision of classical Athenians.[65]

The Acropolis complex was not the only site transformed by Athenian builders in the 440s and 430s. In the western quarter of the city, plainly visible from the

Acropolis, rose the temple of Hephaestus, patron of craftsmen and the deity thought to work the forge of the gods. Today this beautiful building remains almost intact, making it the best-preserved classical temple in Greece. In other parts of Attica, too, new temples appeared. At Sunium, at the peninsula's southern tip, rose a shrine to the sea god, Poseidon. And at Eleusis, near the border with Megara, the Athenians erected another impressive work by Ictinus, the Hall of Mysteries, in honor of Demeter, goddess of plants and fertility. Viewing the results of Pericles' building program as a whole, Plutarch left behind the following impression, a verdict that has endured to the present:

Phidias's towering statue of the goddess Athena stands within the Parthenon's cella, or main room.

The Temple of Hephaestos, standing largely intact after more than two thousand years, is still a prominent sight when viewed from the summit of the Acropolis.

It is this, above all, which makes Pericles' works an object of wonder to us—the fact that they were created in so short a span, and yet for all time. Each one possessed a beauty which seemed venerable [impressive in old age] the moment it was born, and at the same time a youthful vigor which makes them appear to this day as if they were newly built. A bloom of eternal freshness hovers over these works of his and preserves them from the touch of time.[66]

"Faces of God-like Serenity"

No less impressive than the buildings themselves were the paintings and sculptures that adorned and surrounded them. Because of its open democratic institutions and generous support of arts and culture, Athens attracted craftsmen, artists, and sculptors from all over the Greek world. From the island of Thasos, for example, came the master painter Polygnotus, who revolutionized the art of wall painting in the Periclean age. Polygnotus abandoned the old style, in which human figures were typically pictured in profile and all standing in the same plane. He achieved new heights of realism by painting people from all angles and placing them at varying distances from the viewer. Among his most famous works, none of which have survived, were "The Sack of Troy," adorning a wall in Athens's marketplace, and several large murals in the "Picture Gallery" housed within the

Propylaea on the Acropolis. Many other artists of the day were inspired by his use of the "heroic" style, that is, the portrayal of people as more graceful and beautiful than they actually were.

This stylistic attempt to capture humanity's noble ideal rather than its mundane reality carried over into the discipline of classical sculpture. "From the mastery of movement and anatomy," explains scholar Thomas Craven, Athenian sculptors "proceeded to ideal forms and faces—to the creation of figures, male and female, beyond those produced by nature . . . marbles which reveal living flesh within the polished surfaces, faces of godlike serenity."[67]

The greatest sculptor of the age was Phidias, who trained and supervised many other gifted young sculptors. Before his friend Pericles summoned him to work on the Parthenon, Phidias had already distinguished himself by a number of great works. One of these was the Athena Promachos, a thirty-foot-high bronze statue of Athens's patron deity fashioned from the Persian weapons captured at the Battle of Marathon. Standing between the Erechthium and the Propylaea on the summit of the Acropolis, this statue was an unforgettable sight: its spear tip and helmet reflected sparkles of sunlight that could be seen from far out at sea.

Phidias created perhaps his two most memorable works for the Parthenon. The first was the 525-foot-long frieze, or band of sculptured figures, that wound around the upper perimeter of the building. According to Charles Robinson:

The scene represents the Panathenaic [all-Athens] procession, a mid-summer festival, when the best young blood of Athens, youths on horseback and afoot, girls with [sacrificial] offerings, brought a new robe for the old wooden statue of Athena on the Acropolis. At the east end of the Parthenon, over the main entrance, are gathered the gods of [Mount] Olympus [thought to be their home], giving their blessing to this purely local celebration.[68]

Clearly, this work was much too huge in scope for Phidias to have done it alone. Most likely he designed it and then supervised its completion by seventy or more sculptors. His other great masterwork was another colossal statue of the goddess—the Athena Parthenos. This one, some

A modern drawing of the master sculptor Phidias, whose fifth-century B.C. statues and friezes remain among the finest ever produced.

A section from Phidias's Parthenon frieze captures the amazing detail, dramatic energy, and noble spirit that characterized the whole Acropolis complex.

forty feet high and composed of wood, ivory, and over twenty-five hundred pounds of pure gold, stood inside the cella, or main room, of the temple. Unfortunately, this undoubtedly awesome creation has not survived. In fact, writes John Crow:

> Not a single statue by the great Phidias, master sculptor of the Periclean age, has survived, but what remains of the . . . frieze on the Parthenon and on the small temple of Nike [goddess of victory], done under his direction . . . may be the highest point that sculpture in marble has attained in the entire history of man.[69]

Excellence Seldom Equaled, Never Surpassed

The Periclean age also witnessed a surge of great literature, most notably in the fields of drama and history. Hundreds of plays were written for the relatively new medium of the theater, which had originated in Athens in the late sixth century B.C. Over time, theaters and playwrights sprang up in many other Greek poleis and, centuries later, in Rome and modern Europe. But the dramas produced in Athens during the fifth century remain standards of excellence. For power, in-

Athenian Theater Tickets

Athenian playgoers usually arrived at the theater shortly after dawn and watched four or five plays, which in total lasted up to eight hours. This entire day's entertainment was surprisingly inexpensive by today's standards, as classical scholar Paul Roche explains in The Orestes Plays of Aeschylus.

"Admission was free at first; later by ticket. In the time of Demosthenes (fourth century B.C.) a seat cost two obols a day [an obol equaled one-sixth of a drachma, and an average Greek worker earned about two drachmas per day]. Since it was a civic duty to attend the festivals Pericles established a theater fund (the Theoric Fund) from which the poor citizens were given money to buy tickets. A great many of these tickets or tokens have been unearthed, ranging from the end of the fifth century B.C. until well on into the early Christian era. They look rather like coins and are of bronze, lead, ivory, bone, and terracotta [baked clay]. There were special seats for distinguished persons. . . . It is probable that men and women sat in different parts of the auditorium, and that courtesans [prostitutes] sat away from the other women."

sight, and originality, they have been seldom equaled and certainly never surpassed up to the present day.

Athenian theatrical production was the highlight of a yearly religious festival—the City Dionysia, dedicated to Dionysus, god of fertility. As described by Robinson:

The scene of the festival was the Theater of Dionysus, an open-air structure on the south slope of the . . . Acropolis. The auditorium seated approximately eighteen thousand persons [at its greatest expansion]. At its foot was a level, circular area, called the orchestra, where the action took place. No matter what their role, the actors . . . were men, who wore masks to set the general type of character they portrayed, for in a theater of this size facial expressions and other nuances [details] of acting would be lost. . . . In the middle of the orchestra stood the *thymele*, an altar sacred to Dionysus and garlanded for the occasion. On its steps sat musicians, for there was much singing and dancing in a Greek play. Across the orchestra from the auditorium rose the scene building [*skene*], which served as a simple background for the production.[70]

There were both tragic plays and comic plays. Tragedy, most often based on sweeping and serious themes of history and mythology, was the first and most popular dramatic form. The three masters of

fifth-century tragedy were Aeschylus, Sophocles, and Euripides. The high point of Aeschylus's career was in the 470s and 460s, the early phase of the Fifty Years. In addition to *The Persians*—a depiction of the Greek victory over Persia, and the world's oldest surviving tragedy—Aeschylus wrote about ninety plays. He also won the grand dramatic prize of the City Dionysia at least thirteen times.

Aeschylus's younger colleague, Sophocles, hailing from the town of Colonus in Attica, won the prize no less than eighteen times. Only 7 of his 123 plays have survived, but fortunately for humanity one is

Aeschylus (left), one of the world's greatest playwrights; and the Theater of Dionysus (as it appeared in the second century B.C.), where his works were first presented.

Oedipus the King, generally acknowledged to be the greatest tragedy ever written.

Euripides was less popular in his own time than either Aeschylus or Sophocles. This was partly because the themes he explored questioned traditional moral values and often shocked or disturbed audiences. One of his most famous plays,

Medea, depicts the title character mercilessly killing her young children.

Comedy, always filled with slapstick gags, many of them crude and vulgar by today's standards, was also popular. Most of the comic plays involved music and dancing and so, says classical scholar Lionel Casson, were

The Universality of Suffering

In this excerpt from his essay "Euripides and His Age," in Three Great Plays of Euripides, *renowned classical scholar Rex Warner explains how the ancient dramatist earned the nickname of "most tragic poet."*

"He [Euripides] lived in an age of startling discovery and invention and, in particular, an age of questioning during which all established notions of thought and behavior came in for examination and criticism. He also lived in an age of almost continuous warfare. Most of his plays were produced during the years of the long struggle between Athens and Sparta [the Peloponnesian War], and it would appear that Euripides, more than any other writer of antiquity [ancient times], was moved by the horrors and wastages of war and by the sufferings of its victims. . . . War may produce . . . the most spectacular examples of human suffering, and in wartime . . . with the collapse of normal [civilized] restraint, man's nature reveals a peculiar savagery. Yet if there were no wars there would still be suffering. Moreover a slave, a woman, an ordinary man can suffer as much as a king. It is in showing the individuality and also the universality of suffering that Euripides deserves the title of 'the most tragic poet.'"

Euripides' plays, written in one of Athens's most turbulent periods, questioned traditional social customs and values.

In this re-creation of a scene from a Greek comedy, the master of the house is blissfully unaware of the doings of his mischievous slave. Note the use of masks to denote stock character types.

more like our musicals than our [regular] comedies; they contained set pieces [musical numbers] which the chorus sang and danced. . . . When the chorus engaged in dialogue with an actor, its leader delivered the lines by himself, and in ordinary speech . . . but the whole body could, at any moment, break into brief bursts of song.[71]

The best-loved comic playwright of the age was Aristophanes. In hilarious comedies such as *Clouds*, *Frogs*, and *Lysistrata*, he poked fun at politicians, social institutions, and rich and poor people alike.

Another great literary figure of the age was Herodotus, who later became known as the "father of history." He was born in Ionia, but was early attracted to the intellectual community in Athens, which became his second home. In 443 he emigrated with other Athenian cleruchs to Italian Thurii, where he died just after the end of the Fifty Years. His *Histories*, a

chronicle of the Greek and Persian wars, was the world's first known history text. Writes Michael Grant:

> His collection and presentation of material is as astonishing a feat as anything else that was achieved by anyone during the [fifth] century. The mass of the evidence he provides contains a great deal that is accurate . . . and entitle[s] him to be called the pioneer, not only of history, but also of . . . anthropology and archaeology.[72]

Unlike many of his later imitators, Herodotus did not limit himself to military and political events. His work also provides a wealth of ethnic and cultural information about many ancient peoples. In the opening lines, he stated his ambitious goal, one he then ably proceeded to fulfill: "to preserve the memory of the past by putting on record the astonishing achievements both of our own and of

A True Scientist

Part of what made Herodotus a good historian was his open mind. Noted scholar C. M. Bowra elaborates in this excerpt from his excellent study of Greek culture, The Greek Experience.

"His experience confirmed Herodotus in a natural openness of mind. Though he rejects some stories because they offend his sense of probability . . . it is characteristic of him that he gives in detail some stories about which he is himself skeptical. A signal [obvious] example of this is the circumnavigation of [sailing around] Africa by Phoenicians sent by the [Egyptian] Pharaoh Necho. The details which he gives, notably that at a certain point the sun 'rose on their right hand,' confirm the truth of the story. Once he felt he knew his way with a topic, he was not afraid to indulge in speculations. . . . Of these the most remarkable is his sense of the length of historic and prehistoric time. He was bound by no dogma [rigid traditional views] about the date of creation, and when he saw the alluvial [silt, or soil] deposits of the Nile in the Egyptian Delta, he compared them with five similar cases in the Aegean and ended by suggesting that, if the Nile were to reverse its course and flow into the Red Sea, it would take ten or twenty thousand years to fill it with soil. . . . It was his ability and willingness to welcome new facts and to see their importance that made him a true scientist."

Herodotus was the world's first known historian and therefore is often referred to as the "father of history." His great historical study contains much valuable information about the Mediterranean lands and peoples of his time.

other peoples; and more particularly, to show how they came into conflict."[73]

His Authority Had Grown Too Great

Encouraged by Pericles, writers such as Herodotus, Aristophanes, and Euripides, and artists like Polygnotus, Phidias, and Ictinus propelled Athens, and with it Greece, to its cultural zenith. Yet despite the heights to which Pericles had taken the city, new opponents arose against him. Afraid to risk a direct attack on the powerful, popular leader, they tried to discredit him by prosecuting his famous associates. Among these were Phidias, the philosopher Anaxagoras, and Pericles' mistress, Aspasia, all of whom where charged with corrupt behavior of one kind or another. Aspasia was acquitted and Anaxagoras had only to pay a small fine, but Phidias was not so lucky. According to Plutarch, "Phidias was cast into prison and there he fell sick and died. According to some accounts he was poisoned by his enemies in an attempt to blacken Pericles' name still further."[74]

But as had happened in the past, this newest drive to topple Pericles failed, for his popularity and authority by now had grown too great. Part of this authority derived from his building projects. They not only beautified the city, but also provided enough jobs virtually to eliminate unemployment. His imposing authority also sprang from his image as a tough-minded imperial governor who kept a tight rein on Athenian subject states around the Aegean sphere.

Pericles bolstered this image in an incident that began in 440 B.C. when two Ionian members of Athens's empire, Samos and Miletus, began quarreling over control of another city. Pericles quickly stepped in and settled the argument in the favor of Miletus. To further demonstrate Athenian authority, he tossed out Samos's ruling oligarchs and replaced them with Athenian-style democrats. Samos then made the fatal mistake of rebelling and reinstating its oligarchy. Pericles, says J. B. Bury,

> sailed speedily back to Samos and invested [besieged] it with a large fleet. . . . [Almost] 200 warships now blockaded Samos, and at the end of nine months the city surrendered. The Samians [had] to pull down their walls, to surrender their ships, and pay a war indemnity. . . . They became subject to Athens [once more] and were obliged to furnish soldiers to her armies.[75]

Meanwhile, Athens continued to set up new cleruchies on foreign coasts. These and similar warlike and ambitious moves did not go unnoticed in the Peloponnesus, where fear and envy of Athens were alive and well. Hatred of Athenian "arrogance" was smoldering. Soon it would ignite into a deadly inferno that would engulf all of Greece.

6 The War No One Wanted: A Sudden End to a Glorious Age

That Athens and Sparta would eventually come to death blows was perhaps inevitable. By the mid-430s B.C., the differences between their societies, governments, philosophies, and goals formed a vast gulf of resentment, alienation, and distrust. Each city-state firmly believed that it and its way of life should be supreme in Greece. Leaders on both sides, including Pericles, came to see the Thirty Years Peace only as a temporary postponement of hostilities. It seemed to many Greeks that the truce had remained intact so far only because of the Spartans' notorious slowness to take action. Increasingly, then, these leaders resigned themselves to the idea that the treaty could not and would not last the whole thirty years and that all-out war between Athens and Sparta was probably unavoidable.

Even more ominous was the certainty that Greece's two most powerful states would not be fighting such a war alone. A clear battle line between their two huge leagues of allies was already being drawn. According to historian H. D. F. Kitto:

> The Greek world was now divided. On the one side was the Athenian empire, which men openly called a "tyranny"; on the other, Sparta, the Peloponnesian League, and a number of states

This famous bust of Pericles shows him wearing a helmet, probably to hide his peculiarly elongated head, a trait described by ancient historians.

(notably in Boeotia) that sympathized with Sparta: the first group strong at sea, the second strong on land . . . Athens favoring, even insisting on, democratic constitutions among her allies, the other group favoring oligarchies.[76]

With tensions increasing steadily, each new quarrel that occurred in the Greek sphere, no matter how small, seemed greatly magnified in importance. In such matters one league could be counted on immediately to condemn the other, as when the Peloponnesians denounced Athens's subjugation of the Samian rebels in 439. This hostile atmosphere made Greece like a powder keg waiting for a spark to set it off. But though just about everybody realized that a major armed confrontation was coming, no one foresaw its devastating scope and tragic consequences. No one could have guessed that the conflict would bring about Pericles' downfall, the end of the Fifty Years, and the exhaustion and cultural decline of all the city-states.

"They Will Strike Without Mercy"

The long-range cause of the great war between the Greek leagues, of course, was the rivalry and mutual hatred that had been building for many decades between the Athenian and Spartan spheres. But in the dangerous political climate of the 430s B.C., most people did not take the long view. Concentrating on more recent and breaking events, most Greeks, even many of Athens's allies, saw Athenian ambition and aggression as the chief causes of rising tensions. In a speech to Spartan leaders shortly before the outbreak of the war, a delegation of Corinthians summed up the general anti-Athenian feeling of the day. Chiding the Spartans for their slowness to act against the Athenians, the envoys stated:

> Time after time we have warned you of the harm which the Athenians would do to us. . . . We know the path by which the Athenians gradually encroach upon their neighbors. While they think that you are too dull to observe them, they are less venturesome; but when they see that you are consciously overlooking their aggressions, they will strike without mercy. . . . You have never fully considered what manner of men these Athenians are with whom you will have to fight, and how utterly unlike yourselves. They are innovators, equally quick in the conception and in the execution of every plan; while you are careful only to keep what you have and [are] uninventive. . . . They are resolute, and you are dilatory [slow to act]; they are always abroad and you are always at home. . . . It is their nature neither to be at peace themselves nor to allow peace to other men.[77]

The bold, angry, and anxious tone of the Corinthians' speech was motivated by a recent series of insults and armed clashes. These incidents between Corinth and Athens turned out to be the immediate cause of the war, the long-awaited spark that ignited the powder keg. The trouble had begun on the island of Corcyra, located off Greece's northwestern coast. Corcyra, an oligarchy, was a Corinthian colony with which Corinth had

The Resolute Athenians

In his famous chronicle of the Peloponnesian War, Thucydides provided a lengthy reconstruction of the speech in which the Corinthian envoys denounced Athens to Sparta's leaders. In this well-known excerpt, the Corinthians compare the "audacious" Athenians to the "uninventive" Spartans.

"You have never fully considered what manner of men these Athenians are with whom you will have to fight, and how utterly unlike yourselves. They are innovators, equally quick in the conception and in the execution of every plan; while you are careful only to keep what you have and [are] uninventive; in action you do not even go as far as you need. They are audacious beyond their strength; they run risks which policy would condemn; and in the midst of dangers, they are full of hope. Whereas it is your nature to act more feebly than your power allows, in forming your policy not even to rely on certainties, and when dangers arise, to think you will never be delivered from them. They are resolute, and you are dilatory [slow to act]; they are always abroad, and you are always at home. For they think they may gain something by leaving their homes; but you are afraid that any new enterprise may imperil what you have already. When conquerors they pursue their victory to the utmost; when defeated, they give as little ground as possible. . . . In all these activities they wear themselves out with exertions and dangers throughout their entire lives. None enjoy their good things less because they are always seeking for more."

long maintained a lively trade via the Gulf of Corinth. In 435 a civil war erupted between Corcyrean democrats and oligarchs; when the tide in the fighting turned in favor of the democrats, the oligarchs appealed to the mother polis, itself an oligarchy, for aid. Corinth readily sent a small squadron of warships, but the democrats defeated it.

The scope of the crisis then rapidly widened. The indignant Corinthians immediately prepared to send a large fleet of 150 triremes. Realizing that they had little chance against this force, the Corcyrean democrats in desperation begged Athens, Greece's acknowledged champion of democracy, for help. Pericles and the other *strategoi*, seeing another chance to expand their influence and empire, complied, and in 433 a combined force of Athenian and Corcyrean warships handed Corinth another defeat. This was too much for the Corinthians, whose naval and economic rivalry with Athens was already decades old. They appealed to Sparta, demanding that the only other military superpower in the Greek world mobilize its army at last and rid Greece of the insolent Athenians once and for all. The Corinthians told King Archidamus and other Spartan leaders:

> In the face of such a rival city, Spartans, you persist in doing nothing. . . . Let your procrastination [putting things off] end here; assist your allies . . . to whom your word is pledged, by invading Attica at once. Do not betray friends and kindred to their worst enemies or drive the rest of us in despair to seek the alliance of others.[78]

The Megarian Crisis

War now seemed imminent, yet still the Spartans did not act. This was undoubtedly because Archidamus, despite his mistrust of Athens, sincerely wanted to keep his country out of a destructive war. Showing much less reserve and caution, Pericles convinced his countrymen that another show of Athenian power would make the Peloponnesians even less likely to challenge Athens. The Athenians in 432 B.C. imposed a trade embargo on their neighbor, Megara, which had once more become a Spartan ally. The embargo prohibited the Megarians from dealing at any port controlled by or allied to Athens. Since Athens controlled nearly all the Aegean coasts, Megara was cut off from nearly all but the inadequate trickle of food and goods it received by land.

As the months rolled by and the Megarians began to starve, all eyes in the Greek world focused on Athens and Sparta. Many Greeks, a growing number of Athenians among them, worried that war might break out at any time. They urged Pericles to call off the embargo and blamed him for escalating tensions between the leagues. Plutarch pointed out:

> It seems likely that the Athenians might have avoided war . . . if only they could have been persuaded to lift their embargo against the Megarians and come to terms with them. And since it was Pericles who opposed this solution more strongly than anyone else and urged the people to persist in their hostility toward the Megarians, it was he alone that was held responsible for the war.[79]

The increasing criticism of Pericles' handling of the crisis was aptly illustrated by the way comic writers poked fun at his policy. In his play *Acharnians*, Aristophanes daringly had one of his characters spout the lines:

> For then, in wrath, Olympian Pericles
> Thundered and fumed, and frustrated
>   Greece,
> Enacting laws which ran like
>   drinking-songs:
> *That the [embargoed] Megarians*
>   *presently depart*
> *From earth and Sea, the mainland, and the*
>   *mart [markets].*[80]

With Pericles stubbornly holding firm, the burning question on everyone's lips was: Would the Spartans finally act? Archidamus was still reluctant to move. Plutarch described how he "strove to appease his allies and bring about a peaceful settlement of most of their grievances [against Athens]."[81] But Sparta's council of elders, regarding the Megarian crisis as the last straw, exercised their right by Spartan law to override his authority. They declared that Athens's embargo against Megara was a breach of the Thirty Years Peace because it violated the promise the parties had made to stay out of each other's sphere. And so, in 431 B.C., after only fifteen years, the peace was shattered. The war that no one wanted but everyone expected at last became a reality.

Formulating Strategies

What came to be called the Peloponnesian War proved to be the most destructive conflict in Greek history, partly because it involved nearly every Greek polis. Sparta's major allies were Corinth and most of the other Peloponnesian states, Megara, and several Boeotian poleis led by Thebes and Phocis. On Athens's side were Corcyra, most of the Aegean islands and Ionian cities, and the many Athenian colonies in the Mediterranean region.

From the start, it was clear that the league commanded by Sparta was principally a land power and that led by Athens a sea power. And this set of circumstances was reflected in the combatants' initial strategies. Sparta's plan was to march a huge army of Spartan and allied hoplites directly into Attica and lay waste to the countryside, thereby spreading fear and chaos. This, it was hoped, would induce the Athenians to surrender in short order, since the Spartans were, as usual, uncomfortable with the idea of a long, drawn-out conflict. If the Athenians sent out their hoplites, all the better. As everyone knew, they had little or no chance against the

Spartans in a land fight. With these factors in mind, in May 431 Archidamus, now resigned to the idea that fighting was the only realistic option, led a large army into Attica. Although Plutarch recorded that these forces numbered 60,000, a more reliable figure is 35,000, of which no more than 3,000 to 4,000 were Spartan hoplites. About 11,000 were Boeotians and the rest Peloponnesian League allies.

While the invaders commenced wrecking farmhouses and burning crops, Pericles ordered the whole population of Attica to retreat behind the Long Walls. This was part of the Athenian strategy, which acknowledged that trying to defeat the Spartan army would be foolhardy. Instead, the plan was to take advantage of Athens's control of the sea. Safe behind the city's massive walls, the people would be well supplied by its cargo ships and in the meantime its warships would attack enemy towns on the coasts of the Peloponnesus. Pericles, comments J. B. Bury,

> adopted the strategy of "exhaustion," as it has been called—the strategy which consists largely in maneuvering [around the enemy]. . . . The more we reflect on the conditions of the struggle and the nature of the Athenian resources, the more fully will the plan of Pericles approve itself as the strategy uniquely suitable to the circumstances.[82]

But not all Athenians recognized the wisdom of the plan. Pericles had to defend his strategy to a gathering of distraught citizens who were understandably horrified at the prospect of Spartans continuing to ravage their homeland. "They may do damage to some part of our lands," he said, but that will not prevent us from sailing to the Peloponnesus and there building forts against them and defending them with our navy, which is our strong arm. . . . If they attack our country by land, we shall attack theirs by sea; and the devastation of part of the Peloponnesus will be a very different thing from that of all Attica. For they, if they want fresh territory, must take it by arms; whereas we have abundance of land both in the islands and on the continent [mainland]; such is the power which command of the sea gives. . . . Do not mourn for houses and lands, but for men; it is men who acquire property, but property does not provide men. . . . We must be aware . . . that war is inevitable; and the more willing we are to accept this, the less hard will our enemies press us. Remember that the greatest honors are to be won by men and states where dangers are greatest.[83]

At first, Pericles' plan seemed to work. Although the Peloponnesian host kept up its rampage through the countryside all

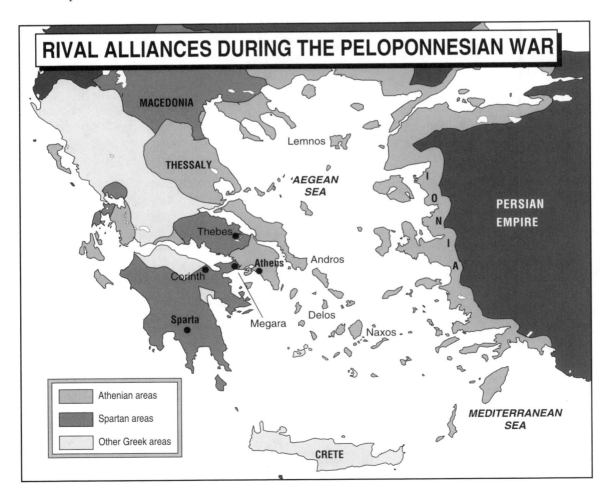

RIVAL ALLIANCES DURING THE PELOPONNESIAN WAR

MACEDONIA

THESSALY

Lemnos

AEGEAN SEA

IONIA

PERSIAN EMPIRE

Thebes

Athens

Andros

Corinth

Sparta

Megara

Delos

Naxos

Athenian areas

Spartan areas

Other Greek areas

MEDITERRANEAN SEA

CRETE

Huddled Together in Shacks

Plutarch devoted only a few lines to the plague that struck Athens in 430 B.C., unlike Thucydides, who described the epidemic in graphic detail. As this excerpt from his Life of Pericles *shows, Plutarch's version emphasized the effect of the plague crisis on Pericles' political career.*

"For now the plague fell upon the Athenians and devoured the flower of their manhood and their strength. It afflicted them not only in body but also in spirit, so that they raved against Pericles and tried to ruin him, just as a man in a fit of delirium will attack his physician or his father. They were urged on by his personal enemies, who convinced them that the plague was caused by the herding together of the country folk into the city. Here, in the summer months, many of them lived huddled in shacks and stifling tents and were forced to lead an inactive indoor life, instead of being in the pure open air of the country, as they were accustomed. The man responsible for all this, they said, was Pericles: because of the war he had compelled the country people to crowd inside the walls, and he had then given them no employment, but left them penned up like cattle to infect each other, without providing them with any relief or change of quarters."

---

summer, in the winter the invaders departed Attica. Their return to the welcome warmth of their own homes allowed the Athenians to leave the shelter of the Long Walls and begin rebuilding. In the spring of 430 B.C., the invaders returned as expected. In response, the Athenians retreated again behind their walls, this time confident that by following Pericles' plan they would eventually wear the enemy down.

However, the Athenian plan had not anticipated the attack of a very different and ultimately more deadly enemy. A violent disease epidemic suddenly struck the city. The historian Thucydides, who witnessed the disaster firsthand, later described the plague, which remains unidentified:

The disease is said to have begun south of Egypt in Ethiopia; from there it descended into Egypt and Lybia; and after spreading over the greater part of the Persian empire, suddenly fell upon Athens. It first attacked the inhabitants of the Piraeus . . . [and] afterwards reached the upper city [Athens], and then the mortality became far greater. . . . The victims . . . were seized first with violent heats in the head and with redness and burning of the eyes. Internally, the throat and the tongue at once became blood-red, and the breath abnormal and fetid [foul]. . . . Vomiting, producing violent convulsions, attacked most of the sufferers. . . . The disorder which had originally settled in the head passed gradually through the whole body and . . . would often seize the extremities and leave its mark, attacking the genitals, fingers and toes; and many escaped with the loss of these, some with the loss of their eyes.[84]

But many more victims died. In the epidemic's first few months alone, Athens lost more than 20 percent of its population.

The Athenian people, terrified and frustrated, looked for someone to blame. They suddenly turned on Pericles, saying that he had been the one who had involved them in the dreadful war in the first place. "They were urged on by his personal enemies," recorded Plutarch, "who convinced them that the plague was caused by the herding together of the country folk into the city. Here, in the summer months, many of them lived huddled in shacks and stifling tents and were forced to lead an inactive indoor life."[85] Forced once more to defend himself, Pericles, by his right as a *strategos*, convened a meeting of the Assembly. He declared:

> I was expecting this outburst of anger against me, for I can see its causes. . . . What sort of man am I to provoke your anger? I believe that I am second to none in devising . . . a sound policy, a lover of my country, and incorruptible. . . . The resolution in favor of war was your own as much as mine. . . . The visitations of heaven [i.e., the plague] should be borne as inevitable, the sufferings inflicted by the enemy [should

be met] with courage. This has always been the spirit of Athens, and should not die out in you now. You should recognize that our city has the greatest name in all the world because she does not yield to misfortunes.[86]

The Right Leader at the Right Time

Initially, a majority of the citizens rejected Pericles' defense and sought to punish him. Since creating bad policy was not a crime, they accused him of embezzling money, which everyone realized was a preposterous charge against one of the wealthiest men in the Greek world. They then levied a fine against him and stripped him of his rank. However, they soon discovered to their dismay that Athens possessed no one else of his caliber to lead them in the war. So after only a few months the fickle Athenians reinstated Pericles in his former position of authority.

As it turned out, all the discord and political bickering came to nothing. As Plutarch recalled:

> Soon after this it appears that Pericles himself caught the plague. In his case it was not a violent or acute attack such as others had suffered, but a kind of dull, lingering fever, which persisted through a number of different symptoms and gradually wasted his bodily strength and undermined his noble spirit.[87]

In 429 B.C., with the war barely two years old, Pericles died, leaving Athens virtually leaderless in the midst of its worst crisis

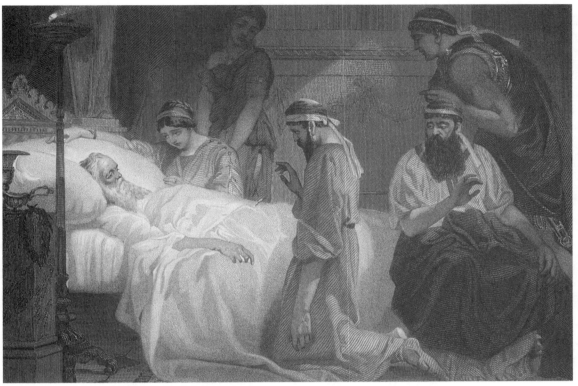

A modern depiction of Pericles on his deathbed. After his passing, Athens entered a downward spiral that eventually led to defeat and ruin.

ever. It is uncertain whether at that moment the people understood the true significance of this loss. In time, though, they would come to the same judgment that Plutarch expressed centuries later. "Pericles deserves our admiration," he wrote, "not only for the sense of justice and serene temper that he preserved amid the many crises and intense personal hatreds which surrounded him, but also for his greatness of spirit."[88]

That spirit had been arrogant and imperialistic, yet at the same time heroic and just. It had been stubborn and at times brutal, but nonetheless cultured and creative. This unique mix of qualities had made Pericles precisely the right leader at the right time to guide his countrymen to greatness. After his passing, life in Greece would never be the same. Their most glorious age had reached a sudden end and their most terrible ordeal was about to begin.

7 The Fall of Athens: Greek Civilization's Great Turning Point

It was perhaps fitting that Pericles' untimely death came at the beginning of the long Peloponnesian War. He and his policies had symbolized and driven the great age of the *Pentekontaetia*. With the outbreak of the war, that turbulent yet immensely constructive age ground to a halt as the Athenians and other Greeks began to channel their energies into more destructive endeavors. Pericles represented the Greece that was passing away; and his own passing, like the coming of the great war, constituted a milestone. According to H. D. F. Kitto:

> This war was the turning point in the history of the Greek polis. It lasted almost continuously from 431 to 404 B.C.—twenty-seven years of it. . . . Fighting went on in almost every part of the Greek world—all over the Aegean . . . in Boeotia, around the coasts of the Peloponnesus, in northwest Greece, in Sicily . . . and Attica.[89]

Describing the unprecedented devastation and chaos, Thucydides wrote that the struggle inflicted "calamities such as Greece had never known within a like period of time. Never were so many cities captured and depopulated. . . . Never were exile and slaughter more frequent."[90]

In a very real sense, the ravages of the long war drained away the potent energies and creative forces that had driven the Athenians and other Greeks in the momentous fifth century. At war's end, with a new century dawning, the Greek poleis were ruined, exhausted, disillusioned, and more disunited than ever. What was left of Greece was a patchwork of largely tired and timid cities, none of which trusted the others. Therefore, Kitto maintains, the conflict brought "the end of the city-state as a creative force fashioning and fulfilling the lives of all its members."[91] This left Greece as a whole wide open to subjugation by new and stronger enemies.

Thus, the great war of the Greek leagues brought more than the end of Athens's shining moment of greatness in the Periclean age. It also signaled the beginning of the end of classical Greek civilization as the leading political and cultural force in the Mediterranean world. It would be for Greece's conquerors to transmit to the modern world the brilliant legacy of Pericles' time.

The Savagery Continues

At the moment that Pericles died in his bed in 429 B.C., no one in Greece foresaw that the war would drag on for a quarter-century, bringing an enormous amount of death and destruction. Even in Athens, where the plague had taken a terrible toll, most people were confident that the city would recover. The idea that Athens would not remain a great power and rule its vast maritime empire forever was simply unthinkable.

The immediate question, now that Pericles was gone, was whether to continue the war or to sue for peace. Two political factions arose. The first, led by a wealthy citizen named Nicias, who had on occasion served as a *strategos* with Pericles, favored peace. The other group, headed by a politician named Cleon, advocated fighting on until total victory was achieved. Cleon got his way at first because, as Plutarch wrote, he was a more ambitious and forceful leader:

> Cleon commanded a large following because of his practice of "pampering the people and finding jobs for all.". . . Nicias, by contrast, wore an air of gravity which was by no means harsh . . . but was blended with earnestness and caution. . . . Pericles had governed Athens above all by virtue of his natural superiority and the force of his eloquence. . . . Nicias, on the other hand, lacked these qualities. . . . He could not command either the opportunism or that knack of telling the people what they wanted to hear with which Cleon constantly humored the Athenian citizenry.[92]

As the war dragged on, the two sides stuck, more or less, to their original strategies. Each spring the Athenians retreated behind the Long Walls and watched as the enemy pillaged the surrounding country-

side. At the same time, the Athenian navy maintained continuous raids on enemy merchant ships and coastal communities. Occasionally, one side or the other scored a major success. In 427, for example, the Spartans besieged and sacked Athens's longtime ally Plataea and, in a cruel and unnecessary gesture, slaughtered or enslaved all the inhabitants. Two years later Athens achieved a degree of revenge by capturing and occupying the town of Pylos, on the western coast of the Peloponnesus.

The Idea of Peace

The savagery continued until 422, when both Cleon and Sparta's best military general, Brasidas, were killed in battle. Cleon's violent death seemed to emphasize the wrongness of his militant policy, and now Nicias saw his chance to sway his own people toward the idea of peace. "Nicias's name was on everyone's lips," wrote Plutarch in his *Life of Nicias:*

> Nicias quickly grasped the fact that the Spartans had for some time been anxious for peace, while the Athenians no longer had the same appetite for the war. . . . Nicias therefore put forth all his efforts to reconcile them and to deliver the other Greek states from the evils of war. . . . Having discussed in this spirit every point at issue, they [the various leaders] concluded the peace. . . . People [believed] that Nicias was the man responsible for the peace, as Pericles had been for the war. . . . So to this day that armistice is known as the Peace of Nicias.[93]

But it soon became clear that the optimistic Peace of Nicias was doomed to fail. Hatred of Athens still ran deep among many of Sparta's allies, especially Corinth and Thebes. Both poleis held grudges for the many abuses and embarrassments they had suffered at the hands of the Athenians, and now they sought revenge. There would be no peace, they insisted, until they had brought Athens to its knees.

Another reason the peace failed was the sudden ascendancy in Athens of a capable and personable politician named Alcibiades. According to Plutarch, "He was a man of many strong passions, but none of them was stronger than the desire to gain the upper hand over his rivals."[94] Once he had done so and won the hearts of the people, Alcibiades showed his true stripes. Though gifted with a brilliant mind, good looks, and many admirable talents, he was arrogant, unprincipled, and determined to create a reputation for himself as a great war hero. He concluded that the best way to achieve this goal was to revive hostilities with the Spartans.

Alcibiades' Plan

To this end, Alcibiades persuaded Elis, Mantinea, and Argos, among the most prominent members of the Peloponnesian League, to defect to Athens's side. This act, wrote Plutarch, "shook almost all the states of the Peloponnesus and set them against one another."[95] Alcibiades' plan proved successful. The Spartans quickly crushed the rebels and then turned their wrath once more on Athens.

In time, the new Athenian war leader suggested a bold change in his country's strategy. Instead of hiding behind the city walls and trying to wear down the enemy, he said, the Athenians should go on the offensive. He proposed sending a military expedition to Sicily, to conquer the powerful Greek city of Syracuse. This would bring Athens vast new supplies of wealth, foodstuffs, and troops, against which Sparta and its allies would swiftly go down to defeat. Ignoring the advice of Nicias and his own supporters, who thought the venture too risky, Alcibiades rammed the proposal through the Assembly. The mighty force, totaling perhaps 140 warships and over eight thousand troops, sailed for Syracuse in 415 B.C. To foster political unity, the people placed Nicias, against his wishes, in joint command with Alcibiades.

Alcibiades, the "Benedict Arnold of Greece," sold out his country to the enemy at the height of his power and influence.

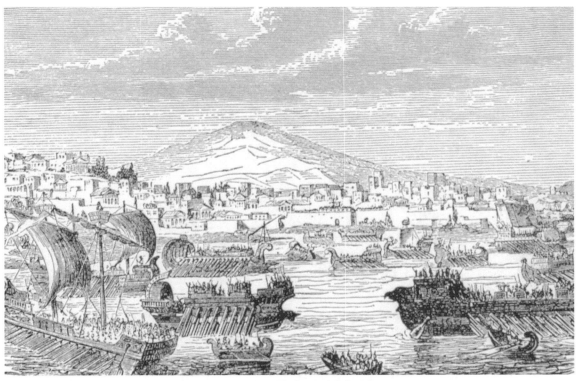

The massive Athenian fleet menaces Syracuse. After Alcibiades' defection to Sparta, these forces came under the command of Nicias, a second-rate military leader.

But the expedition was doomed, in no small part because Alcibiades turned out to be a traitor. Shortly after the ships departed, the opponents of the ambitious commander accused him of having defaced some religious statues in Athens and recalled him for trial. Instead of denying, or at least facing the charges, he fled and took refuge in Sparta. His surprised countrymen were stricken with grief and rage, especially after they learned of what he had told a Greek who asked him why he did not trust his fellow Athenians. "Where my life is at stake," he replied, "I wouldn't trust my own mother not to mistake a black pebble for a white one when she casts her vote."[96] Alcibiades promptly convinced the Spartans to send their own expedition to Sicily and help the Syracusans defeat the Athenians.

Alcibiades' treachery left Nicias, a mediocre military leader, in charge of the Syracusan expedition. After many months of delays, strategic blunders, and minor defeats, the Athenians suffered the worst military disaster in their long history. In the autumn of 413, Nicias lost most of his fleet. Immediately afterward, a combined force of Spartan and Syracusan hoplites trapped and completely defeated his land army. The Syracusans then executed Nicias and his officers and condemned

Spartan and Syracusan hoplites inflict heavy casualties as they pursue the retreating remnants of the Athenian army across the countryside near Syracuse. Nearly all of the defeated Athenians were killed or enslaved.

the other survivors to hellish slavery in Sicily's stone quarries.

Disaster and Surrender

Incredibly, even after such horrendous losses, Athens fought on. Straining its resources to the limit, the once-great city-state built new fleets and attempted to stem a tide of battle that was steadily turning against it. But this herculean effort was in vain. In 405, the Spartans, who had recently built their very first fleet of warships, cornered an Athenian fleet at Aegospotami, near the mouth of the Hellespont. Seeing a chance to cut off Athens's precious grain route to the Black Sea, the Spartan commander, Lysander, ordered an attack. As Plutarch described it, when the trumpet on the admiral's flagship sounded the attack, the ships moved forward, while at the same time the land forces raced along the shore to seize the headland. At this point on the Hellespont the two continents are less than two miles apart, and the rowers pulled with such a will that they fairly ate up the distance. Conon, the Athenian general, was the first to notice Lysander's fleet bearing down upon them. He instantly shouted out orders to embark and, in an agony of distress at the impending disaster, commanded, implored, and drove his crews to man their ships. . . . The [Athenian] men, as they ran up unarmed and in straggling order, were slaughtered in a vain attempt to rescue their ships, or else, if they retreated inland, the enemy disembarked and cut them down as they fled. Lysander took 3,000 prisoners, including the generals, and captured the entire fleet, with the exception of the state galley, the *Paralus*.[97]

Clearly, the loss of the grain route constituted a disaster of the greatest magnitude for Athens. Since it was no longer

Poetry Buys Freedom

Placement in Sicily's stone quarries usually constituted a death sentence for the survivors of the Athenian Syracusan expedition. But a little-known and fascinating footnote to this episode, recorded in Plutarch's Life of Nicias, *suggests that a fortunate few were saved by a kind of literary miracle.*

"Most of the Athenian prisoners perished in the quarries from sickness and from their wretched diet, for they were given no more than a pint of meal [ground grain] and a half pint of water a day. A number were stolen away and sold as slaves. . . . [However], a few were rescued because of their knowledge of [the works of] Euripides [the playwright], for it seems that the Sicilians were more devoted to his poetry than any other Greeks living outside the mother country. Even the smallest fragments of his verses were learned from every stranger who set foot on the island, and they took delight in exchanging these quotations with one another. At any rate there is a tradition that many of the Athenian soldiers who returned home safely visited Euripides to thank him for their deliverance which they owed to his poetry. Some of them told him that they had been given their freedom in return for teaching their masters all they could remember of his works, while others, when they took to flight after the final battle, had been given food and water for reciting some of his lyrics."

possible to feed the masses of citizens camped in idleness behind the Long Walls, there was no longer any credible way to carry on the war effort. The Greek historian Xenophon captured the people's anguish on the night the *Paralus*, after escaping Aegospotami, arrived at Piraeus:

As the news of the disaster was told, one man passed it on to another, and a sound of wailing arose and extended first from the Piraeus, then along the Long Walls until it reached the city. That night no one slept. They mourned for the lost [soldiers], but more still for their own fate. They thought that they themselves would now be dealt with as they had dealt with others.[98]

The subsequent turn of events showed that the civilians' fears were well founded. In exhaustion and despair, the Athenians surrendered in 404 and immediately faced a series of harsh humiliations. The victorious Spartans and their allies forced them to tear down the Long Walls and to abolish their much-cherished democracy. Sparta then installed an oligarchy composed of thirty conservative Athenians, who soon became known as the "Thirty Tyrants." The leader of the new government of Athens was a spiteful character named Critias, one of Alcibiades' former colleagues. The Thirty promptly initiated a reign of terror in which many democrats and their sympathizers were murdered or driven from Attica.

After Athens had endured much bloodshed and heartache, Sparta eventually allowed it to restore its democracy. But it was plain that the great age of Athenian political and cultural supremacy was over. Not only in Athens but in the rest of Greece as well, it was as if the people had lost their constructive and creative energies. Even the Spartans, the victors of the war, were exhausted and soon proved unable to maintain their newly acquired status as the dominant polis in all of Greece. On the one hand they longed to return to their traditional isolation. On the other they lacked the political skills and experience to administer so large an area.

The Bloodshed Continues

As a result, Greece lapsed into still more chaos and bloodshed. The major city-states, seemingly having failed to learn the lesson of the great war, skirmished with one another again in largely vain attempts to gain supremacy. One result of this fighting was Sparta's demise. In 371 B.C., at Leuctra in southern Boeotia, Thebes, led by a brilliant general named Epaminondas, delivered the long-invincible Spartan phalanx a crushing defeat. This forever eliminated Sparta as a major Greek power.

As another and more fateful result of all this strife and chaos, the Greek heartland now lay weak and vulnerable to outside attack. That inevitable assault came from Macedonia, a formerly backward and uncultured region of extreme northern Greece. In the mid-fourth century, Macedonia's King Philip II organized the region's disunited tribes into a powerful kingdom. As Michael Grant explains,

This achievement had become possible because Philip was the leading general of the day and made his army more formidable than any the

As musicians play, the Spartans force the Athenians to tear down the Long Walls after Athens's surrender. The city's cherished democracy was also dismantled.

Mediterranean world had ever seen. Heavy cavalry, exceptionally well-trained, transformed land warfare by operating in wedge-shaped formations of his own invention, and the Macedonian infantry, drawn up in a phalanx of novel flexibility and depth, were armed with spears and pikes twice as long as those carried by the [classical] Greeks.[99]

Philip had his eyes on Athens, Thebes, Corinth, and the other splendid commercial and cultural centers of southern Greece. On August 4, 338, his lethal "Macedonian phalanx" easily won the day against a larger army of Thebans, Athenians, and other Greeks at Chaeronea in central Boeotia.

Soon afterward, Philip was assassinated. But his son Alexander, who would

Members of the lethal Macedonian phalanx brandish their long pikes, called sarissas. A mass of thousands of these pikes presented an enemy army with a frightening and impenetrable wall of metal spear points.

later be called "the great," maintained Macedonia's grip on Greece. Alexander was both ambitious and daring. In 334 he led a Greek army into Persia and in only ten years managed to carve out an immense empire that stretched from Macedonia to India. Then he died unexpectedly, possibly of malaria, at the age of thirty-three.

Alexander's legacy to Greece turned out to be a new round of civil strife, political disorder, and human suffering. After his passing his generals fought each other in long bloody wars and ended up establishing several Greek-ruled kingdoms in the eastern Mediterranean and western Asia. Continuing rivalry among these

states made the Greeks still more disunited and war-weary. It is hardly surprising, therefore, that they eventually fell prey to another outside power.

A Lesson for All Times

That power was Rome, which had recently emerged as the strongest power in the western Mediterranean sphere. In the second century B.C., the Roman army, which was even more formidable than either Philip's or Alexander's, conquered the Greek kingdoms in the eastern sphere. Fortunately for later generations, the Romans took an instant liking to Greek culture. They readily borrowed many Greek customs, ideas, and artistic and architectural styles and adapted them to their own use. In the process, the Romans absorbed the great literary works produced in the Periclean age and kept alive the memory of the Greek leaders described in these works. Men such as Themistocles, Aristides, Cimon, and Pericles came to be seen as heroic figures on a par with Rome's own most revered heroes. This is why Plutarch and other Roman writers so avidly recorded the deeds of these long-dead Greeks.

When, in the fifth century A.D., Roman civilization too declined, eventually to slide into oblivion, it left behind a rich

The kingdom of Alexander the Great fell apart soon after his untimely death at the age of thirty-three.

cultural legacy to the small European kingdoms that succeeded it. Part of this legacy included memories of the priceless cultural riches of Periclean Athens. And in this way, these riches, over time, became part of the very fabric of the modern Western world. "One need only look closely at our own language, our political institutions, and our culture," comments Pierre Leveque, "to discover to what extent the Greek experience lives on."[100]

Greece's Legacy

Greek architecture, especially the temples and other buildings erected during the Fifty Years under Pericles' guidance, offers a clear example of this surviving Greek legacy. The exteriors of thousands of modern government and university buildings, courthouses, and libraries bear the familiar rows of Greek columns topped by a triangular pediment. These structures owe their inspiration most of all to the Parthenon and its sister temples on the Acropolis, the mightiest surviving symbol of Pericles and his times. John Miliadis remarks:

> This moment—the great thirty years of Pericles—brought the Acropolis from time into eternity and gave it forever its universality. No other work of man has been so national in its roots, and so international in its fruit. None was more the product of its own age, and none has meant so much to all future ages. Nothing is less a relic of the past, and more perennially present.[101]

No less important was the legacy of Greek democracy, brought to its fullest flower in the Periclean age. As John Crow puts it:

The Athenian democracy born under Cleisthenes [and expanded under Pericles] endured for almost two centuries. The Roman Republic was fashioned [partly] in imitation of it, and so in greater or lesser degree were all democratic and republican forms of government of a later date. The founders of our republic [the United States] were particularly inspired by it, especially the trio of distinguished writ-

The Thirty and the Reign of Terror

Later generations of Athenians never forgot the frightening reign of terror imposed by the Thirty Tyrants, the Spartan-backed oligarchs who briefly ruled Athens after its surrender in 404 B.C. This excerpt describing one of the city's darkest episodes is from Hellenica *by the Athenian historian Xenophon.*

"At Athens the Thirty were chosen directly after the demolition of the Long Walls and the walls of the Piraeus. Though they were chosen to frame laws for a new constitution they kept putting things off. No laws were framed or published, and meanwhile they appointed members of the Council and other magistrates just as they saw fit. Their first measure was to arrest and put on trial for their lives all who were generally known to have made a living during the time of the democracy by acting as informers and [who] had made a practice of attacking the aristocrats. . . . Next, however, the Thirty began to consider how they could get the power to do exactly what they liked with the state. They sent [some of their number] to Sparta to persuade Lysander to support their request that a Spartan garrison [of troops] should be sent just until, so they said, they had got rid of the 'criminals' and had established a new constitution. . . . Lysander agreed and . . . when they got their garrison . . . they began to arrest all whom they wished to arrest. And now it was no longer a question of the so-called 'criminals' or of people whom no one had heard of. Those arrested now were the people who, in the view of the Thirty, were the least likely to submit to being pushed out of politics and who could count on the greatest support if they chose to take action [against the tyrants]. . . . So more and more people were put to death, and put to death unjustly, and . . . many citizens . . . wondered what the state was coming to."

The imposing colonnades and triangular pediments on the wings of the U.S. Capitol in Washington, D.C., are a modern living tribute to Greek temple architecture.

ers, [Alexander] Hamilton, [James] Madison, and [John] Jay, whose clarion [clear] call to [democratic] union . . . clearly reveals that they had imbibed at [drunk from] the Attic spring.[102]

One of the most important aspects of the legacy of the Periclean age is often the most overlooked or ignored. It is the political history lesson the events of that age provide for people today and indeed for all societies in all times. In its great and shining moment of power and glory, Athens made a fatal mistake. It might have worked to find a way to live in peace with its neighbors, gain true and friendly allies, and thereby ensure its control of a strong and united Greece. That formidable nation might have withstood the Roman on-

slaught and gone on to become the chief colonizer of Europe and perhaps eventually the world. But instead, Athens pursued the course of greed and imperialism, and in so doing planted the seeds of its own destruction.

The universal lesson of the Periclean age, then, is that the most powerful and splendid of nations can be toppled by greed, arrogance, hatred, and revenge. Pericles had been right in his now famous prediction about the eternal quality of Athenian art and culture. "Future ages will wonder at us," he declared, "as the present age wonders at us now."[103] But what he did not foresee was that his country's failure to achieve peace and unity with its neighbors would ensure that the leaders of those future ages would not be Greek.

Notes

Introduction: The Worst Along with the Best

1. Plutarch, *Life of Pericles*, in *The Rise and Fall of Athens: Nine Greek Lives*. Translated by Ian Scott-Kilvert. New York: Penguin Books, 1960, p. 183.
2. Victor Ehrenberg, *From Solon to Socrates: Greek History and Civilization During the Sixth and Fifth Centuries B.C.* London: Methuen, 1968, p. 226.
3. Ehrenberg, *From Solon to Socrates*, p. 226.
4. Pericles, *Funeral Oration*, quoted in Thucydides, *The Peloponnesian Wars*. Translated by Benjamin Jowett. New York: Washington Square Press, 1963, p. 67.
5. Thucydides, *The Peloponnesian Wars*, p. 83.

Chapter 1: Seeds of Bitter Rivalry: The Long Prelude to the Classic Age

6. Rodney Castleden, *Minoans: Life in Bronze Age Crete*. New York: Routledge, 1990, pp. 32–33.
7. Michael Wood, *The Search for the Trojan War*. New York: New American Library, 1985, p. 247.
8. Wood, *The Search for the Trojan War*, p. 249.
9. Pierre Leveque, *The Birth of Greece*. New York: Harry N. Abrams, 1994, pp. 51–52.
10. John A. Crow, *Greece: The Magic Spring*. New York: Harper & Row, 1970, p. 102.
11. Charles Alexander Robinson Jr., *Athens in the Age of Pericles*. Norman: University of Oklahoma Press, 1959, p. 6.
12. Thucydides, *The Peloponnesian Wars*, p. 3.
13. Plutarch, *Life of Solon*, in *The Rise and Fall of Athens*, pp. 54–55.
14. Quoted in Plutarch, *Life of Solon*, in *The Rise and Fall of Athens*, p. 60.
15. Thucydides, *The Peloponnesian Wars*, p. 6.
16. Thucydides, *The Peloponnesian Wars*, p. 8.
17. Peter Connolly, *The Greek Armies*. Morristown, NJ: Silver Burdett, 1979, p. 26.
18. J. B. Bury, *A History of Greece to the Death of Alexander the Great*. New York: Random House, n.d., pp. 205–206.
19. Herodotus, *The Histories*. Translated by Aubrey de Sélincourt. New York: Penguin Books, 1972, p. 441.
20. Crow, *Greece*, p. 128.
21. Thucydides, *The Peloponnesian Wars*, pp. 10–11.

Chapter 2: From Alliance to Empire: The Aegean Becomes an Athenian Lake

22. Thucydides, *The Peloponnesian Wars*, p. 11.
23. Crow, *Greece*, p. 117.
24. Donald Kagan, *The Outbreak of the Peloponnesian War*. Ithaca, NY: Cornell University Press, 1969, pp. 39–40.
25. Thucydides, *The Peloponnesian Wars*, p. 39.
26. Plutarch, *Life of Cimon*, in *The Rise and Fall of Athens*, pp. 145–146.
27. Plutarch, *Life of Cimon*, in *The Rise and Fall of Athens*, p. 158.
28. Ehrenberg, *From Solon to Socrates*, pp. 195–196.
29. Thucydides, *The Peloponnesian Wars*, p. 40.
30. Quoted in Kagan, *The Outbreak of the Peloponnesian War*, p. 127.
31. Plutarch, *Life of Cimon*, in *The Rise and Fall of Athens*, pp. 158–159.
32. Plutarch, *Life of Cimon*, in *The Rise and Fall of Athens*, p. 159.

33. Kagan, *The Outbreak of the Peloponnesian War*, p. 72.

Chapter 3: An Amazing Energy: Athens's Struggle to Maintain Supremacy

34. Peter Levi, *Atlas of the Greek World*. New York: Facts On File, 1984, p. 140.

35. Levi, *Atlas of the Greek World*, p. 140.

36. Russell Meiggs, *The Athenian Empire*. Oxford: Clarendon Press, 1972, pp. 205–206.

37. Bury, *A History of Greece*, p. 338–339.

38. Meiggs, *The Athenian Empire*, p. 259.

39. Ehrenberg, *From Solon to Socrates*, p. 205.

40. Bury, *A History of Greece*, p. 337.

41. Quoted in Plutarch, *Life of Pericles*, in *The Rise and Fall of Athens*, p. 173.

42. Quoted in Bury, *A History of Greece*, p. 339.

43. Kagan, *The Outbreak of the Peloponnesian War*, p. 87.

44. Plutarch, *Life of Pericles*, in *The Rise and Fall of Athens*, p. 175.

45. Plutarch, *Life of Cimon*, in *The Rise and Fall of Athens*, p. 160.

46. Meiggs, *The Athenian Empire*, p. 97.

47. Plutarch, *Life of Pericles*, in *The Rise and Fall of Athens*, pp. 177–178.

48. Plutarch, *Life of Pericles*, in *The Rise and Fall of Athens*, p. 175.

Chapter 4: Democracy and Imperialism: A City Thrown Open to the World

49. Diodorus, *Historical Library*, quoted in Kagan, *The Outbreak of the Peloponnesian War*, pp. 107–108.

50. Plutarch, *Life of Pericles*, in *The Rise and Fall of Athens*, p. 171.

51. Plutarch, *Life of Pericles*, in *The Rise and Fall of Athens*, p. 176.

52. Quoted in Leveque, *The Birth of Greece*, pp. 158–159.

53. Michael Grant, *The Ancient Mediterranean*. New York: Penguin Books, 1969, pp. 203–204.

54. Quoted in Thucydides, *The Peloponnesian Wars*, pp. 67–69.

55. Kagan, *The Outbreak of the Peloponnesian War*, pp. 136–142.

56. Robinson, *Athens in the Age of Pericles*, p. 33.

57. Bury, *A History of Greece*, p. 334.

58. Robinson, *Athens in the Age of Pericles*, p. 90.

59. Kagan, *The Outbreak of the Peloponnesian War*, p. 119.

60. Plutarch, *Life of Pericles*, in *The Rise and Fall of Athens*, p. 182.

Chapter 5: The Classic Achievement: Athens Reaches Its Cultural Zenith

61. Grant, *The Ancient Mediterranean*, p. 204.

62. Plutarch, *Life of Pericles*, in *The Rise and Fall of Athens*, p. 177.

63. Plutarch, *Life of Pericles*, in *The Rise and Fall of Athens*, pp. 178–179.

64. Crow, *Greece*, pp. 186–187.

65. John Miliadis, *The Acropolis*. Athens: M. Pechlivanidis, n.d., p. 52.

66. Plutarch, *Life of Pericles*, in *The Rise and Fall of Athens*, p. 179.

67. Thomas Craven, *The Pocket Book of Greek Art*. New York: Pocket Books, 1950, p. 37.

68. Robinson, *Athens in the Age of Pericles*, pp. 57–58.

69. Crow, *Greece*, p. 173.

70. Robinson, *Athens in the Age of Pericles*, p. 61.

71. Lionel Casson, *Masters of Ancient Comedy*. New York: Macmillan, 1960, pp. 5–6.

72. Michael Grant, *The Classical Greeks*. New York: Charles Scribner's Sons, 1989, p. 78.

73. Herodotus, *The Histories*, p. 41.

74. Plutarch, *Life of Pericles*, in *The Rise and Fall of Athens*, p. 198.

75. Bury, *A History of Greece*, pp. 366–367.

Chapter 6: The War No One Wanted: A Sudden End to a Glorious Age

76. H. D. F. Kitto, *The Greeks*. Baltimore: Penguin Books, 1951, p. 136.

77. Quoted in Thucydides, *The Peloponnesian Wars*, pp. 25–28.

78. Quoted in Thucydides, *The Peloponnesian Wars*, pp. 28–29.

79. Plutarch, *Life of Pericles*, in *The Rise and Fall of Athens*, p. 196.

80. Aristophanes, *Acharnians,* in Moses Hadas, ed., *The Complete Plays of Aristophanes*. New York: Bantam Books, 1962, p. 30.

81. Plutarch, *Life of Pericles*, in *The Rise and Fall of Athens*, p. 196.

82. Bury, *A History of Greece*, p. 383.

83. Quoted in Thucydides, *The Peloponnesian Wars*, pp. 47–49.

84. Thucydides, *The Peloponnesian Wars*, pp. 73–74.

85. Plutarch, *Life of Pericles*, in *The Rise and Fall of Athens*, p. 201.

86. Quoted in Thucydides, *The Peloponnesian Wars*, pp. 78–82.

87. Plutarch, *Life of Pericles*, in *The Rise and Fall of Athens*, p. 204.

88. Plutarch, *Life of Pericles*, in *The Rise and Fall of Athens*, p. 205.

Chapter 7: The Fall of Athens: Greek Civilization's Great Turning Point

89. Kitto, *The Greeks*, p. 136.

90. Thucydides, *The Peloponnesian Wars*, p. 13.

91. Kitto, *The Greeks*, p. 152.

92. Plutarch, *Life of Nicias*, in *The Rise and Fall of Athens*, pp. 209–210.

93. Plutarch, *Life of Nicias*, in *The Rise and Fall of Athens*, pp. 217–219.

94. Plutarch, *Life of Alcibiades*, in *The Rise and Fall of Athens*, p. 246.

95. Plutarch, *Life of Alcibiades*, in *The Rise and Fall of Athens*, p. 257.

96. Quoted in Plutarch, *Life of Alcibiades*, in *The Rise and Fall of Athens*, p. 265.

97. Plutarch, *Life of Lysander*, in *The Rise and Fall of Athens*, p. 296.

98. Xenophon, *Hellenica* (published as *A History of My Times*). Translated by Rex Warner. New York: Penguin Books, 1979, p. 104.

99. Grant, *The Ancient Mediterranean*, p. 212.

100. Leveque, *The Birth of Greece*, p. 127.

101. Miliadis, *The Acropolis*, p. 6.

102. Crow, *Greece*, pp. 109–110.

103. Pericles, *Funeral Oration*, quoted in Thucydides, *The Peloponnesian Wars*, p. 69.

For Further Reading

Isaac Asimov, *The Greeks: A Great Adventure*. Boston: Houghton Mifflin, 1965. An excellent, entertaining overview of the ancient Greeks, with an emphasis on their importance to later cultures.

Peter Connolly, *The Greek Armies*. Morristown, NJ: Silver Burdett, 1979. A fine, detailed study of Greek armor, weapons, and battle tactics and their evolution over the centuries in ancient Greece. Filled with colorful, appropriate illustrations. Highly recommended.

———, *The Legend of Odysseus*. New York: Oxford University Press, 1988. A useful and entertaining book, retelling the story of the Trojan War and its aftermath. Supplemented by numerous illustrations and many excellent and accurate sidebars explaining various aspects of Mycenaean civilization.

Rhoda A. Hendricks, translator, *Classical Gods and Heroes*. New York: Morrow Quill, 1974. A collection of easy-to-read translations of famous Greek myths and tales, as originally told by ancient Greek and Roman writers, including Homer, Hesiod, Pindar, Ovid, and Sophocles.

Homer, the *Iliad*, retold by Barbara Leonie Picard. New York: Oxford University Press, 1960; and the *Odyssey*, retold by Barbara Leonie Picard. New York: Oxford University Press, 1952. Simple, entertaining versions of the epic tales that helped define the classical Greeks' heroic outlook and religious ideas. Translated and presented specifically for young readers.

Perry Scott King, *Pericles*. New York: Chelsea House, 1988. A short but useful overview of the Periclean age and the man who came to symbolize it.

Don Nardo, *Ancient Greece*. San Diego, CA: Lucent Books, 1994. A general overview of Greek history, providing a broader context for understanding the events and achievements of the Periclean age.

———, *The Battle of Marathon*. San Diego, CA: Lucent Books, 1996. This volume provides detailed coverage of the political and military events in Greece and Persia in the sixth and early fifth centuries B.C., culminating in the Greek and Persian Wars, which directly preceded and had an important bearing on the Periclean age.

———, *Life in Ancient Greece*. San Diego, CA: Lucent Books, 1996. This detailed study of classical Greek social, cultural, political, and religious customs, habits, and ideas constitutes a useful supplement to historical volumes on Greece.

Susan Peach and Anne Millard, *The Greeks*. London: Usborne, 1990. A general overview of the history, culture, and myths of ancient Greece. Filled with fine, historically accurate color illustrations.

Major Works Consulted

J. B. Bury, *A History of Greece.* New York: Random House, n.d. Though somewhat dated, this work, originally composed in 1900 by one of the great classical historians, remains among the most thoughtful and well-researched overviews of ancient Greek history.

John A. Crow, *Greece: The Magic Spring.* New York: Harper & Row, 1970. A very well written survey of Greek culture and ideas, covering major historical events as well as art, literature, philosophy, and religion.

Victor Ehrenberg, *From Solon to Socrates: Greek History and Civilization During the Sixth and Fifth Centuries B.C.* London: Methuen, 1968. An insightful, scholarly study of the period, including the Periclean age.

Michael Grant, *The Rise of the Greeks.* New York: Macmillan, 1987. One of the finest and most prolific of modern classical historians, Grant delivers a masterful, highly detailed, and scholarly study of Greek civilization, focusing one by one on the important city-states. Founding, development, and contributions are explored.

Herodotus, *The Histories.* Translated by Aubrey de Sélincourt. New York: Penguin Books, 1972. A fine translation of the efforts of the man known as the father of history in his own words, to put "on record the astonishing achievements both of our own and of other peoples; and more particularly, to show how they came into conflict." A priceless source for memorable details about ancient Greek culture and attitudes.

Donald Kagan, *The Outbreak of the Peloponnesian War.* Ithaca, NY: Cornell University Press, 1969. A masterful survey of the division of the Greek world into Athenian and Spartan camps and other political and military developments during the Periclean age, leading up to the war itself. One of the best sources available on the subject.

Pierre Leveque, *The Birth of Greece.* New York: Harry N. Abrams, 1994. A commendable introduction to ancient Greek history and culture, with insightful commentary. Filled with first-rate photos, drawings, reproductions of paintings and sculptures, and re-creations of temples and other buildings in their original form. Highly recommended.

Russell Meiggs, *The Athenian Empire.* Oxford: Clarendon Press, 1972. A fine, detailed study of the rise and fall of the Athenian empire, beginning with the foundation of the Delian League and ending with Athens's defeat in the climax of the Peloponnesian War. Will appeal primarily to serious scholars.

Plutarch, *Lives of the Noble Grecians and Romans,* excerpted in *The Rise and Fall of Athens: Nine Greek Lives.* Translated by Ian Scott-Kilvert. New York: Penguin Books, 1960. This useful volume contains clear, easy-to-read translations of the following famous biographies by this ancient writer: Theseus, Solon, Themistocles, Aristides, Cimon, Pericles, Nicias, Alcibiades, and Lysander.

Charles Alexander Robinson Jr., *Athens in the Age of Pericles.* Norman: University of Oklahoma Press, 1959. A thoughtful look at the Periclean age. Lengthy discussions of Greek democracy and politics are supplemented by several long primary source quotations.

Thucydides, *The Peloponnesian Wars.* Translated by Benjamin Jowett. New York: Washington Square Press, 1963. Even after more than two thousand years, the master historian's telling of the events surrounding the wars that ended Greece's golden age remains fascinating reading. Highly recommended for all.

Additional Works Consulted

John Boardman, *Greek Art*. New York: Thames and Hudson, 1985.

C. M. Bowra, *The Greek Experience*. New York: New American Library, 1957.

James Henry Breasted, *Ancient Times: A History of the Early World*. New York: Ginn, 1944.

Lionel Casson, *Masters of Ancient Comedy*. New York: Macmillan, 1960.

Rodney Castleden, *Minoans: Life in Bronze Age Crete*. New York: Routledge, 1990.

Thomas Craven, *The Pocket Book of Greek Art*. New York: Pocket Books, 1950.

M. I. Finley, *The Ancient Greeks*. New York: Penguin Books, 1977.

———, *The Greek Historians*. New York: Viking, 1959.

W. G. Forest, *The Emergence of Greek Democracy: The Character of Greek Politics, 800–400 B.C.* London: Weidenfeld and Nicolson, 1966.

———, *A History of Sparta, 950–192 B.C.* New York: Norton, 1968.

Michael Grant, *The Ancient Mediterranean*. New York: Penguin Books, 1969.

———, *The Classical Greeks*. New York: Charles Scribner's Sons, 1989.

———, *A Social History of Greece and Rome*. New York: Charles Scribner's Sons, 1992.

Peter Green, *The Parthenon*. New York: Newsweek Book Division, 1973.

Moses Hadas, *The Greek Ideal and Its Survival*. New York: Harper & Row, 1960.

Moses Hadas, ed., *The Complete Plays of Aristophanes*. New York: Bantam Books, 1962.

Victor David Hanson, *The Western Way of War: Infantry Battle in Classical Greece*. New York: Oxford University Press, 1989.

H. D. F. Kitto, *The Greeks*. Baltimore: Penguin Books, 1951.

Bernard Knox, ed., *The Norton Book of Classical Literature*. New York: Norton, 1993.

Peter Levi, *Atlas of the Greek World*. New York: Facts On File, 1984.

John Miliadis, *The Acropolis*. Athens: M. Pechlivanidis, n.d.

Gilbert Murray, *The Literature of Ancient Greece*. Chicago: University of Chicago Press, 1956.

Plutarch, *Lives of the Noble Grecians and Romans*. Translated by John Dryden. New York: Random House, 1932.

Betty Radice, *Who's Who in the Ancient World: A Handbook to the Survivors of the Greek and Roman Classics*. New York: Penguin Books, 1973.

C. E. Robinson, *Everyday Life in Ancient Greece*. Oxford: Clarendon Press, 1968.

Paul Roche, *The Orestes Plays of Aeschylus*. New York: New American Library, 1962.

Charles Van Doren, *A History of Knowledge, Past, Present, and Future*. New York: Ballantine Books, 1991.

Rex Warner, *Three Great Plays of Euripides*. New York: New American Library, 1958.

Leonard Whibley, ed., *A Companion to Greek Studies*. New York: Hafner, 1963.

Michael Wood, *The Search for the Trojan War*. New York: New American Library, 1985.

Xenophon, *Hellenica* (published as *A History of My Times*). Translated by Rex Warner. New York: Penguin Books, 1979.

Index

Picture Credits

Cover photo: Stock Montage, Inc.

Archive Photos, 87

The Bettmann Archive, 24, 29, 34, 41, 54, 57, 58, 59, 61, 67, 70, 77

Library of Congress, 17, 18, 79

North Wind Picture Archives, 10, 15, 16, 20, 22, 26, 27, 32, 37, 38, 49, 53, 65, 68, 69, 72, 74 (bottom), 75, 76, 90, 91, 92, 97

Stock Montage, Inc., 39, 45, 48, 71, 74 (top), 95, 96

About the Author

Don Nardo is an award-winning author whose more than seventy books cover a wide range of topics ranging from science and the environment to flying saucers and voodoo. His main field, however, is history. Among his modern historical studies are overviews of five of America's wars; *Braving the New World*, the saga of African Americans in colonial times; and biographies of Thomas Jefferson, Joseph Smith, and Franklin D. Roosevelt. Mr. Nardo's specialty is the ancient world, especially classical Greece and Rome, about which, in addition to this volume on the Periclean age, he has written: *The Battle of Marathon, The Battle of Zama, Life in Ancient Greece, Greek and Roman Theater, The Roman Republic, The Roman Empire, The Punic Wars, Caesar's Conquest of Gaul*, and many others. Mr. Nardo also dabbles periodically in orchestral composition, oil painting, screenwriting, and film directing. He lives with his wife Christine on Cape Cod, Massachusetts.